"We cannot both say and explain what we say."

Gilles Deleuze

ALSO BY RÉMI BOYER:

Freemasonry as a Way of Awakening

MASK
CLOAK
SILENCE

Martinism as a Way of Awakening

Rémi Boyer

Rose Circle Publications
Bayonne NJ
2021

Mask Cloak Silence:
Martinism as a Way of Awakening

A warm thanks to Howard Doe for his many useful and insightful improvements to the translation draft.

ISBN: 978-1-947907-13-3
Library of Congress Control Number: 2021903238

Originally published in French as *Masque, manteau, silence: Le martinisme comme voie d'éveil* by Éditions de la Tarente, 2017. latarente.fr

Cover painting: *O Paracleto* by Lima de Freitas, acrylic on canvas, 1991. Courtesy of Helle Hartvig de Freitas.

Book design and layout by Michael Sanborn, TextArc LLC. michael@textarc.net

Rose Circle Publications
P.O. Box 854
Bayonne, NJ 07002, U.S.A.
www.rosecirclebooks.com

to EivLys
to Marie
to Axel

to Claude Bruley,
to Lima de Freitas,
to Robert Amadou,
to Armand Toussaint,
to Jean-Louis Larroque,

and the third generation of Past Masters who,
after Martines de Pasqually, Louis-Claude de Saint-Martin,
Jean-Baptiste Willermoz and, later,
Papus and the Companions of Hierophany,
gave Martinism,
with and following Robert Ambelain,
a radiance never before attained.

Contents

Foreword

I am honored to be asked to write a Preface to this important translation of a seminal French book by the renowned esoteric author and practitioner Rémi Boyer, and I applaud the work which Michael Sanborn is doing to bring a series of important French works to the attention of the English-speaking world.

In 1863, Edward Burton Penny translated the correspondence which passed between the Unknown Philosopher, the nom-de-plume of Louis-Claude de Saint-Martin, and Kirchberger, Baron von Liebistorf, in his work *Theosophic Correspondence.* This work has never been out of print. I can similarly hope that this profound work by Rémi Boyer will be read by students of Saint-Martin and Martinism in the coming centuries.

Indeed, this translation has the singular honor of being perhaps the first book in English on what is called "Martinism." While a number of people, myself included, have sought to translate the original works which led to this Order coming into existence, thereby providing access to source documents which had never before been translated, this book falls into a second category: that of interpreting the ideas and teachings of those original masters.

The French have always prided themselves in their approach to philosophy, from their own great philosophers and thinkers, and the almost stereotypical image of Frenchmen sitting in a café arguing the fine points of thought over a Pernod, absinthe, cognac, or kir, to the immense number of books dedicated to esoteric and symbolic thought which are published every year. And the number of books continues to grow.

This series of books includes Freemasonry, Martinism, and the Rosicrucians (or Rose-Croix), with an appendant volume on the Rectified Scottish Rite. Last year saw the publication in English of Boyer's book on Freemasonry; and this year we see his seminal work on Martinism.

Martinism began as a uniquely French phenomenon, born out of the mind of Saint-Martin, whom it is believed had a small number of like-minded friends, and who also practiced a form of initiation into his system just prior to and after the French Revolution. However, it wasn't until Dr. Gérard Encausse—better known as Papus—in the latter part of the 19th century that the notion of Martinism both became codified into a quasi-Masonic Order, and started flourish both in France and abroad.

While the Order predominantly focused on esoteric theosophy and debate in France, its Anglo-Saxon cousin fared less well. Its first proponent in the United States, Eduard Blitz, wanted to transform it into a traditional Masonic Order with many different Grades. This didn't sit well with Papus and his Supreme Council, whose experience of French Masonry was less than stellar. As a result, the mantle of leadership in the US was passed to Margaret B. Peeke, a populist esoteric writer, which made the overt point that, being led by a woman, the Order most certainly wasn't Masonic. Like the Hermetic Order of the Golden Dawn, the choice of a woman to be a leader in the Order was ahead of its time.

However, the main thing the Order lacked was education, and apart from a series of short lectures on general esoteric knowledge, popularly known as "The Conventicles," little original Martinism education—other than the rituals themselves—ever made it across the "pond."

Meanwhile, scholarship and original thought proceeded apace in France. Such eminent figures as Paul Sédir, Dr. Marc Haven, René Guénon, and many others, later replaced by Robert Ambelain and other luminaries, continued the tradition of writing about the philosophy of the Order; while the historic side was masterfully covered by René le Forestier, Alice Joly, Robert Amadou, and the chair of Esoteric Studies at the Sorbonne, Prof. Antoine Faivre. Now we have Rémi Boyer, Serge Caillet, Jean-Marc Vivenza, and others who keep the flame alive and add to our understanding of this important Masonic, Rosicrucian, Theosophical, and Esoteric tradition.

With such an embarrassment of riches on the French side, it is curious that the English-speaking world lags so far behind in this field of study. Yet we must remember that a society pervaded by philosophical though and esoteric nuance is not exactly an Anglo-Saxon trait, whereas books on "getting rich quick" will always outsell books on critical thinking or self-actualization.

And yet, here we find a book which, for once, focuses on the praxis and the philosophy of Martinism, rather than an academically inclined source document. And I commend it to you, gentle reader!

Herein you will find a French Preface by a man I truly respect in this field: Serge Caillet. This alone is a *tour de force,* which will give the reader new to this field a strong grounding in the subject. As an acknowledged expert in his field, I was honored when my old friend accepted my dedication to him in my translation of Saint-Martin's and Papus' posthumous works in *The Numerical Theosophy of Saint-Martin & Papus.*

The body of the work itself will both inspire and give much food for thought. Providing extracts from the rituals and the commentaries upon the sources, and the inspiration to which they give rise, the work is transcendental, as it is meant to be. It is a glorious synthesis of history, an explanation of the symbolism, and a source of practical ideas which has hitherto been absent in the English-speaking world. Its side journey into Gnosticism and the resurgence of the Cathar Church is particularly informative.

However, it is the appendices which truly move us from theory to practice, and the exercises they contain are to be commended. The book concludes with a bibliography which, while mostly citing the many French works on the subjects, also references an increasing number of books becoming available in English. However, it must be said that most of the books listed are source materials. What we lack is the vast—and growing—library of books in French focused on the praxis of these techniques, and how Martinism is both relevant and critical to a world which seems to have lost its purpose and its place in the universe.

As an experiential book about Martinism and its practices, unique in the English-speaking world, I cannot recommend this book enough.

Piers A. Vaughan
Proprietor of Rose Circle Publications
National Grand Master of the United States of America for the
    Martinist Order of Unknown Philosophers
February 2021

Preface

By Serge Caillet

To Claude Calmels Beaulieux,
in the friendship of the unknown philosopher

*

Martinism

After having designated the illuminist current of the admirers of Louis-Claude de Saint-Martin, called the Unknown Philosopher, the term "Martinism," which was born in the last years of the eighteenth century, covers today different realities, the most classic of which applies to the Martinist orders under the posthumous patronage of Saint-Martin.

However, unlike Martines de Pasqually, who had, in the first part of his career, literally followed the practice of a high ceremonial theurgy in the framework of an initiatory school, Saint-Martin, who took as a second, posthumous, master the Görlitz theosopher Jacob Bœhme, offers intimates, who are his friends and readers, a path stripped of all ritual form. There is no actual Saint-Martinian filiation (it is evident and one begins to know it through saying it and writing it), as Robert Amadou demonstrated, in favor of the filiation of desire which links the Martinists of the nineteenth, twentieth and twenty-first centuries to the Unknown Philosopher of the Enlightenment.

The paradox is that Providence entrusted a young medical student, in the Belle Époque of Occultism, in 1887-1891, with the founding of a small initiatory circle: the Martinist Order, the first of its kind, of a simple ritual form (see the *Cahiers de l'Ordre réservés aux loges régulières et aux initiateurs,* facsimile in "Documents martinistes n° 14," *Cahiers de l'Ordre au temps de Papus,* Paris, Cariscript, 1981). This medical student, as is well known, was called Gérard Encausse, whose name will make him famous to the point that Anatole France had dreamed of entrusting him with a chair of magic at the College de France.

By giving a first assembly and reception ritual to his Martinist Order, which soon surpassed the informal character of a circle of intimates, Papus distanced himself, of course, from the practice and sensibility of Saint-Martin. But the Spirit blows where it wills, and it is up to the Martinists to ensure that the so-called initiation "of Saint-Martin," which goes back only to Papus, as recorded in the annals of history, guides spiritually more and more back to the way of Saint-Martin, which is internal and, therefore, guides back to God alone: "My sect is Providence," says the Unknown Philosopher.

After having admitted me, on May 23, 1994, in the Martinist chain where Robert Ambelain had been received himself, on September 1, 1942, with the ritual analyzed throughout this work, Robert Amadou, whose preference went to the primitive ritual of Papus, reminded me as an aside: "I hope it will help you to go towards God and move on. Otherwise, it is not worth it." And the old master added with a smile: "For titles, if you want, you just have to make some!" Now here, in the form of a joke, are the two paths that offer themselves to contemporary Martinists.

For Martinism, spiritually full of promise, in its present social form, is also capable, and one cannot hide this, of misleading the initiatable by entertaining them. As in other societies considered initiatory, some have found there how to build their own tower of Babel, in the multiplication of ranks, titles, functions, offices, initiations, rituals...

On the other hand, Rémi Boyer's quest testifies to the effectiveness of the Martinist initiation, among other initiations, for his own benefit and for the benefit of men and women of desire gathered around the third generation of companions of the Hierophany. Encouraged by a few of the second generation, among whom Robert Amadou played a leading role, a third generation was indeed emancipated in the 1980s. We were mostly young, as had been our former elders of the Belle Époque, Papus in the lead, and our elders of the years 1940-1960, often gathered around Robert Ambelain.

From the hope of the *Arc-en-ciel* symposia (1987-1989), devised by Rémi Boyer, will be born the Group of Thebès, forced to be suspended due to lack of the required discretion and to misunderstanding. But bases were laid, sites were opened, and prospects were emerging. As for Martinism, there were a few that Robert Amadou then called to the succession (see the conclusion of his preface to my *Sâr Hiéronymus et la FUDOSI,* Paris, Cariscript, 1986, p.13).

With others, Rémi Boyer quickly became one of them. After having been made a member of the Martinist Order of the Knights of Christ, by "a man out of the stream," Armand Toussaint (1895-1994), who had constituted him in Belgium in 1971, he became one of the most active representatives. Similarly, in a completely different genre, the International Center for Martinist Research and Studies (CIREM), founded under the chairmanship of Robert Amadou in 1992, would not have emerged if Rémi Boyer had not assumed the Secretariat General. The publications of CIREM, starting with the thirty-three issues of the first series of its journal, *l'Esprit des choses,* have made no small contribution in recent decades to the study and spread of Martinism. In fact, these peripheral phenomena obscure, in the eyes of many, certain central enterprises, wherein I must first and foremost include the second resurgence of the Order of Knight Masons Elus Coëns of the Universe, certain circumstances of which Rémi Boyer has himself related elsewhere.

* *

An effective ritual

Beyond the varied forms of the rituals of orders in disorder, Rémi Boyer immediately notes the permanence of something that inhabits Martinist temples. How right he is! And this something is conveyed by the ritual.

Thus, with regard to the Martinism of Papus and the principles posed in his *Freemasonry as a Way of Awakening* (Bayonne, NJ: Rose Circle, 2020), the author invites us to consider Martinism as another way of awakening, on the basis of a ritual. He opted for that of Robert Ambelain, who himself based it on an original text of Papus, which was entirely different from that of Blitz-Teder and that of Dimitri Sémélas. This ritual allows the transmission of the sole rank of "unknown superior," by integrating the essential elements of the two previous grades.

That this ritual was effective underground, under the Nazi occupation, and long after the war, in various circumstances, is enough to convince oneself to judge the tree by its fruits! We know moreover with what legitimate pride—and a touch of irony—Robert Ambelain could claim his place in the genealogical tree of many Martinists and many contemporary orders.

The traditional Martinist Order itself has not escaped, via Raymond Bernard, appointed by Ralph M. Lewis for its restoration in France and the French-speaking countries, with the office of Grand Master, in 1959. Prudent, Bernard will be nevertheless initiated at his request, with the greatest discretion, by Marcel Laperruque, a close friend of Robert Ambelain.

A few years earlier, the same Ambelain had transmitted this deposit to almost all the members of the Supreme Council of the Martinist Order awakened by Philippe Encausse, in 1952, and he founded, in 1968, as we know, his Ordre Martiniste Initiatique.

The Ordre Martiniste et Synarchique had hardly gone beyond the stage of a small group, even in Belgium where it was active in the 1930s among the disciples of Emile Dantinne; even in Switzerland, where Dr. Edouard Bertholet collected the legacy on the death of Victor Blanchard. But Louis Bentin developed it in Great Britain, and spread it to Canada where it bore fruit, before returning to France.

Originally, Papus conceived the Martinist initiation as a single grade, which he then split into three, then four, which was then considered to be associated with a rose-cross grade. Nowadays, still more grades have appeared, which root the Martinist form a little more into a land from which it should, on the contrary, gradually be released.

Robert Ambelain had the genius of the ritual (Robert Amadou saw it as one of the reasons for the effectiveness of the first resurgence of the Elus Coëns, in 1942-1943, of which he was its right arm) and he did not spare himself from writing others, which are very beautiful and very useful. This science of ritual Rémi Boyer exploits in turn today, for the benefit of men and women of desire who will discover in Martinism a genuine way of awakening.

This ritual naturally uses the fundamental symbols of Martinism, which are the mask, the cloak, and the cordelier. Now, every symbol, it is said in good theology, is a vehicle. But of what? Having broken away from the use of symbols, Rémi Boyer plays to bring us back to the only real game. What does it matter that his interpretation is not always formally consistent with that of the old, Martines and Saint-Martin in particular? Why should he, in the newfound freedom of their spiritual sons, stick to the form of which nothing is more urgent than to free oneself?

The mistake would be that apprentices wanted to play the master, depriving themselves precisely of the valuable tools at their disposal. However, these tools are formal. These forms must be respected to be effective. May these few introductory lines, as a modest testimony of friendship with Rémi Boyer, stir up in turn the desire of the reader.

*

*   *

The mask is my true face

The mask of the Martinist initiate, as Robert Amadou taught me the day he handed it to me, symbolizes our true face to acquire, which is none other than that of our divine likeness. And the old master quoted the humorist for whom "up to 40 years old, we have the face that our parents gave us; after 40 years, we have the mug we deserve!"

The mask hides indeed my true face, unless it reveals it. The mask hides a secret, just as it reveals a secret, which is that of deification, as *Ignifer* once confided to me on a bench in the Luxembourg garden, where the shadow of Saint-Martin hovered: we become what we think.

Every man is another Christ, proclaims Saint-Martin, and he can accomplish, in the name of Christ, things as great as the Rabbi *Ieschua* of Nazareth, and even greater ones. The mask hides the Christ in me, and he reveals it to anyone who looks at this mask for what it is. From the suffering Christ to the glorious Christ, in short. For this slave mask, worn by every man redeemed by the Word who took the form of the slave in the Incarnation, hides my true face, which is glory.

But this glory, to which I aspire because it is the true hidden nature of my body, of this body which is not mine, but which is also me, this glory not lost but buried, I cannot find only in silence and obliteration. The mask, like every symbol, is not only the sign of this effacement; it is the means, in an interiorization, of a process of abandonment, which begins with my worldly personality, and which will continue, God willing, in a permanent journey from the periphery to the center: to acquire a face to converse with God face to face.

This quest for the center, which is also the axis of the world, as the center is the axis of man, is the quest for the heart, which the admirable Papus has called "the way of the heart," and that Saint-Martin, a century before him, designates as the Internal. By moving from the multiple to the one, or the peripheral numbers to the central numbers, I move away from the Divider and draw closer to the Lord. I leave the world of time little by little to enter the timeless, walking towards eternity, which is my part of the Lord.

Alas, the Divider reigns in all places, since all places belong to him, in his principality. At the school of Martines, Saint-Martin posits in *Les Nombres* that the square of the three elements, which are fire, water and earth, is built around the number five which makes it the center here. For Adam, in whom man has sinned, was mistaken for the center (see how Martines de Pasqually narrates the episode of his temptation in the first sections of the *Treatise on Reintegration*). In him, every fallen man is a center who confuses his own illusory reality with the real. Fallen man has been poisoned, and, according to Karl von Eckartshausen, our blood keeps a record of it, which draws us to this illusory center as a magnet towards its source.

But the Repairer Himself did not succumb to the traps of the Divider (Matthew, 4:1-11), which overturns for man the perverted values. He thus establishes another center of the world by restoring the center of all things, which is the Kingdom to be reached, so distant, because it is within us where no one seeks it.

Since we must change our center, after the square of the elements, let us adopt with Saint-Martin the number four, our intimate number, which is central, while the number three, which designates forms, is a number of circumference. Four, therefore, will be the true center to be reached, as it reveals unity. But two units are not allowed, and to believe it belongs to the illusion of the evil one. How to go from five to four? By abandoning the four, a descent to the top. Christ on the cross thus signs with his blood the act of redemption of man to the Adversary. And the Martinist initiate is another Christ.

The cloak of past masters

From the mask to the cloak, change the symbol, in search of the real. Among the Elus Coëns, the cloak symbolized the office. And *Ignifer* still insisted on the need, also symbolized by the mask, to play our roles. But what role? Beware of playing the master for the one who, according to Jacques Lacan, ignores that he plays! Past masters are our common temporal fathers (the expression is Saint-Martin's in the place of Martines who was the only living master to his knowledge, so he could not do the trick). As such, they are our spiritual fathers only as images of Christ, the only Master (Matthew, 23:8).

The history of Martinism, which is also that of the past masters, has not always been as noble as one would have liked. How could it be otherwise at the periphery of the facts? For these masters are first of all men, and to confound them with saints is a matter of diabolical idolatry. But because these same men are on their way to sanctification, their virtues cover their sins in a new-found verticality. They then offer themselves to our misty eyes as a symbol of a salutary presence, in their function as the first of the roped.

The presence of past masters inhabits the fire that burns in the east, which is also the center. Now, this fire is reminiscent of a certain new fire for which Saint-Martin details the vocation of the organ of the spirit, itself the organ of God. Without it, nothing is possible, as nothing is possible with matter deprived of its principle, which is the axis of the central fire that, according to Martines de Pasqually, is composed of spirits emanating from God.

The central fire of the Martinist, for which the heart is the natural (and therefore supernatural) habitat, also conveys itself to the past masters, all men and women of desire of the same spirit, recognized as such by their brothers and sisters temporarily incarnated. How? To each his spiritual friendships, his intellectual, literary, and emotional ties. The list is therefore not closed; it is open to the beyond, while they go up with us and we go up with them. But the same spirit lives in them, which is fire.

The cloak of fire characterizes the master. But one cloak hides the other. My cloak of flesh hides my cloak of fire, which is also light. For matter is illusory, as is this body of flesh, in which I am wrapped as a cloak. Our reality here below is only an image, which hides the only reality revealed by the absence of God, present in the world in his Sophia, which, from a certain point of view, is also *la Chose* of the Elus Coëns, the gentle Presence of

Our Lord Jesus Christ. The eternal is wrapped in light like a cloak. This cloak, which is His Glory, protects and enlivens us, ensuring His presence in the fallen world; a Presence of God, which is also silence, when the Word is silenced by withdrawing from the world to make room for the Holy Spirit.

Paradoxically, the cloak of the initiate protects the other. But from what? Not some "bad energies" like the New Age yaps in our ears, but from himself, simply. In the image of God whose likeness he longs for, the initiate fades into his cloak, to allow the other to exist. St. Seraphim of Sarov, model of the true man, withdraws from the world into his cell, to accomplish alone the great work of deification. He thus protects himself from the vampirizing world, while protecting the world from him, thereby promoting the pregnancy of the soul and the birth of another Christ. After giving birth, he opens his cell, receives hundreds of souls and drops the cloak, or reveals his true cloak, which is of glory.

Finally, the cloak joins the mask when, as Rémi Boyer reminds us, the prophet Elias veils his face on Mount Horeb. For no one can see God without dying, but the Son, who is in the bosom of the Father, reveals Him to the eyes of man.

*

* *

* *

Two letters and some points

Two simple letters, which are S and I, and six points: such were the germs of Papus's Martinist initiation.

Martines himself designated as "sovereign judges" those holding the rank of Reaux Croix constituting the Sovereign Tribunal of the Order of Knight Masons Elus Coëns of the Universe, while Saint-Martin, after having followed this first school, reveals in *Le*

Crocodile ou la guerre du bien et du mal (1799; new ed., Hildesheim, Olms, 2008) the idealistic existence of this Society of Independents, which lies behind the secret history of the world but appears only in coded form. Further still, the same letters, composing the same symbol, refer to *The Amphitheater of Eternal Wisdom* of Henrich Khunrath (1595), nailing the serpent on the cross. Cagliostro, whom Papus admired along with Master Philippe, also presents the serpent on the Tau, which Jules Doinel, companion of Papus, adopted as a specific symbol of the bishops of his Gnostic Church, which today, even if sometimes misguided, has grown in numbers dramatically.

The curved line of the S recalls, of course, the serpent, while the straight line of the I recalls the tree, or the axis of the world. But the serpent is also the true Lucifer, the Christ, the second Adam. While the first Adam was seduced by the serpentine form of Satan, made into an angel of light mimicking Wisdom, the second Adam is Wisdom, or Wisdom is his consort. But, if the tree is also the cross, the I is not merely the universal symbol that René Guénon studies in *The Symbolism of the Cross* (1931). He first recalls the cross of Calvary and the *mysterium crucis* of Golgotha. For Guénon, who, moreover, condemns all of Papus, the Martinist Order, the associated schools, and the occultism to which they belong, disregards the historical character, and consequently the real nature of, Christianity. Jean Daniélou, once, made the most relevant criticism (see the special issue of *Planète plus*, dedicated to Guénon, in 1970).

In addition to the two letters, the six points which must accompany them find their origin in Saint-Martin (*Les Nombres,* § 20) where they compose the focal point of the famous drawing that the great master of the Martinist Order will adopt as a pentacle. They thus seem to compete with the three Masonic points, by splitting them. But, whatever the initial intention of Papus, the hexad is analyzed differently, of which Raymond Abellio, for example, affirmed the fundamental character, generally underestimated in favor of the triad (*La structure absolue*, 1965).

The letters S. I. mean for Papus "unknown superior." The two associated words have their origins in the famous Templar Rite of Strict Observance, which gave shape to the Rectified Scottish Rite. The latter is in accord with, via Jean-Baptiste Willermoz, the doctrine of Martines de Pasqually. The real Unknown Superior is at first an unknown servant, and recalls Philippe Encausse, who was a model of this kind.

This Unknown Superior, the true Rose-Croix, is by definition a free man. How can one not agree with Rémi Boyer here when he is sad that most Martinist orders have renounced the Free Initiators, by centralization, by politics, or even by Masonic contamination? Charles Détré (Teder), who, in 1913, had adapted in French the very masonic ritual of Édouard Blitz, then Jean Bricaud and some others after them, confused the Masonic framework and the Martinist form, which was a serious error.

For, while the Masonic initiation is given by and in the lodge, it is the initiator alone who confers the Martinist initiation. The Unknown Superior then acts in the name of the Order, but of an Order whose model is none other than the Society of Independents exalted by Saint-Martin in *Le Crocodile*. Better still, Papus wanted the fundamental character of the Free Martinist initiation, from initiate to candidate, to be outside the ordinary social framework.

Let's push the reasoning. Because it is liberatory even more than Freemasonry—except perhaps for marginal Masonic forms, condemned or normalized by bourgeois masonry—Martinism has no other vocation than to train its members out of the Order that they have entered! For better is to come, and this better, which is the quest for the truth and the One who is the Truth, is acquired in freedom. On this point, the thought of Papus is constant, who, just two years before his death, still reminded an anxious correspondent:

"The purpose of the Order is to direct to the Master of Masters those of its members who are judged by the Invisible worthy of reaching this path. The Order did not ask you to take an oath; it did not ask you for money and it wanted to leave you your complete freedom on all the planes.

"Is it not fair that the members of the Order, who have become serious students of the mystical path, personally seek to follow this path? So it is with pleasure that I see those who have finished their time rushing to new sheepfolds thus leaving space for new recruits who will later follow the same path." ("Lettre à un ami démissionnaire de l'Ordre martiniste," *Mysteria*, February 1914, pp. 173-175)

At the school of Master Philippe, which opens, according to Rémi Boyer, one of the narrow doors of Martinism, Papus (after having abandoned, under the influence of Teder, the simple form of a primitive Martinist order for more complex forms) did not vary in the design of his school, which he even seems to have envisioned being dissolved after his death. Does he not thus join Saint-Martin?

A Christian chivalry

Papus from the start imagined the Martinist Order as "a secular Christian chivalry" that is not subservient to any particular Church, even the Gnostic Church, the famous Gnostic churches where Gerard Encausse, his brothers, and his successors were involved to varying degrees. It is thus, we have seen, that he speaks of it two years before being called to God, as an order which must lead to the Master of masters, who is the Christ.

Martinists are therefore free to attach themselves, in a personal capacity, to the Church of their choice. Today, much as yesterday, many, for obvious reasons, come from that of Rome, which Papus and his family did not like, and which didn't like them either. Others opt for small churches, Gnostic, Rosicrucian, old-Catholic or liberal. Since the second half of the twentieth century, others have recognized the Gnostic Church in Orthodox Churches of the East or West, and Robert Amadou, Father Ibrahim, considered the Syrian Church to be the ideal Church of the Martinists. It is also true that John of Kronstadt, a recent saint of the Russian Church, had greeted Master Philippe as a brother, while the bishop of Moscow, a century earlier, had rendered the most positive account of *Of Errors and Truth,* the first work of the Unknown Philosopher.

Outside the Church, what is it for, this Christian chivalry? Once more, who better than Papus could teach us? "In its totality, the Order is above all a school of moral chivalry, striving to develop spirituality in its members through the study of the invisible world and its laws, through the exercise of devotion and intellectual assistance, and through the creation in each mind of a faith which is all the more enduring as it is founded on observation and science" (*Martinezism, Willermozism, Martinism & Freemasonry.* Bayonne, NJ: Rose Circle, p. 46).

All is said. The study of the invisible world sends us back to the Internal Quest of Saint-Martin, since spirits of every kind are in us, bearing the Kingdom of God, which is also the Kingdom of Heaven. Devotion and fraternal assistance bringing together, beyond the doctrine that already unites them, the Martinist Order and the Order of the Beneficent Knights of the Holy City, where *agape* (Saint Paul, 1 Cor. 13:1-3) replaces the primitive worship of Martines de Pasqually. The faith of the modern "fervent Knights of Christ" (Papus, *op. cit.,* p. 103), recalls Clement of Alexandria for whom the crowned faith in gnosis perfects the naked faith.

This new book by Rémi Boyer, disturbing as it should be in its singular approach—and that bothered me too, thank God!— bears witness to that faith, for the use of all Martinists. So make a place for the author, who knows what he is talking about, a place for the mask, for the cloak, a place for the spirit of Hély blowing in silence.

S. C.

Introduction

"I felt and I must confess that there is nothing indispensable for man but what he can and must do without any help from men or circumstances. That is why truth is the simplest and easiest of sciences."

Louis-Claude de Saint-Martin

SHORTLY AFTER THE PUBLICATION of *Freemasonry as a Way of Awakening*,[1] I was asked to write an equivalent book for Martinism in order to clarify the confusing situation that contemporary Martinism was in at the beginning of this millennium. I replied that it wasn't necessary, as Jean-Marc Vivenza,[2] Serge Caillet,[3] and Jean-Louis Ricard,[4] some of the notable names among the "new" specialists in Martinism, through their efforts, their writings, and their communications, further develop the work initiated and already greatly advanced by Robert Amadou. They contribute, each

---

1 *Freemasonry as a Way of Awakening* by Rémi Boyer (Bayonne, NJ: Rose Circle, 2020).

2 Author of the excellent *Le Martinisme. L'enseignement secret des Maîtres* (Paris: Le Mercure Dauphinois, 2006).

3 Serge Caillet, among others, offers a *Cours de martinisme*, available from the Eléazar Institute, www.institut-eleazar.org.

4 Author of a thesis entitled *Régénération et création littéraire chez Louis-Claude de Saint-Martin* and a master's thesis, *Étude sur Le Crocodile ou la guerre du bien et du mal de Louis-Claude de Saint-Martin*, both published by CIREM, BP 08, 58130 Guérigny—France.

in their own way, to set the framework for this amazing and altogether unexpected branch of illuminism.

Louis-Claude de Saint-Martin would no doubt be astonished if he observed all that the term "Martinism" covers today and the breadth of discussion it generates, sometimes going as far as chaos, from quasi-superstitious occultism to high metaphysics.

However, what strikes the noble traveler who, from country to country, from language to language and order to order, travels the Martinist world, is undoubtedly the permanence of the experience revealed by the Martinist ritual, whatever be the language used, the ritual implemented, or even the quality of the implementation. Whether the ritual is performed sloppily or is realized in the perfection of presence in the moment, the "sense" of the Spirit remains. From what or whom is it derived? What is it that dwells in the Martinist temples built everywhere on the planet that cannot be found either in Freemasonry or in the Order of Knight Masons Elus Coëns of the Universe, the two orders of Brotherhood closest to the Martinist Order? Is it not this dimension of the Heart, the special nature of its cardiac pathway, about which has been said and written far more nonsense than truth, even relative truth?

It seemed to me relevant to look in the few symbols specific to Martinism for what characterizes the cardiac axis. The resulting essay does not claim to carry out an exegesis of Martinism. On the contrary, putting aside the intellect, which never liberates, it is a question of showing how the Martinist ritual conveys (with its operators, or despite its operators) a powerful foreshadowing of the freedom of our own original nature.

In this essay, it is presupposed that you already know what the word "Martinism" covers, its history and its stories, the personalities that influenced it or constituted it from Jacob Bœhme, Emmanuel Swedenborg, Martines de Pasqually, Louis-Claude de

Saint-Martin, Jean-Baptiste Willermoz, then later, Papus, Stanislas de Guaita, the Companions of Hierophany, Master Philippe,
and finally, in the twentieth century, the two Roberts: Robert
Ambelain, the operative, and Robert Amadou, the theosopher.

Let us recall briefly,[5] with the latter, what the term "Martinism" covers.

It is initially the Primitive Cult of the Order of Knight Masons
Elus Coëns of the Universe,[6] founded by Martines de Pasqually
(1710 -1774) including Louis-Claude de Saint-Martin, who was the
secretary and probably the best student.

The Theosophy of Louis-Claude de Saint-Martin[7] (1743-1803)
is at the crossroads of two founding experiences: the experience
of a Réau-Croix who successfully realized all Coëns operations,
and the encounter of the work of Jacob Bœhme of which he will
be a translator. Recall that Jacob Bœhme, often described as a
mystic, was also a high-level operative hermeticist.

It is the Masonic system of the Rectified Scottish Rite founded
by Jean-Baptiste Willermoz (1730-1824) from the Templar Strict

---

5   From *Martinisme* by Robert Amadou, 2nd edition revised and expanded (Guérigny, Fr: CIREM, 1997).

6   Two books presented and commented by Robert Amadou are
essential to the understanding of the Primitive Cult: *Les leçons de Lyon
aux élus coëns. Un cours de martinisme au XVIIIe siècle par Louis-Claude
de Saint-Martin, Jean-Jacques Du Roy D'Hauterive, Jean-Baptiste Willermoz,* by Robert and Catherine Amadou, first complete edition published
after the original manuscripts (Paris: Dervy, 1999), and Martines de
Pasqually—*Traité sur la réintégration des êtres dans leur première propriété,
vertu et puissance spirituelle divine,* first authentic edition after the manuscript of Louis-Claude de Saint-Martin, established and presented by
Robert Amadou (Le Tremblay, Fr: Diffusion rosicrucienne, 1995).

7   The complete works of Louis-Claude de Saint-Martin are available at Olms. We draw your attention to the introductions of Robert
Amadou which allow one to better apprehend the thought of the Unknown Philosopher.

Observance,[8] imbued with the doctrine of reintegration by Martines de Pasqually. The Profession and the Grand Profession, the crowns of this system, are a synthesis of the doctrine conveyed by the Primitive Cult.

Finally, it is the Martinist Order, and its many emanations, founded in 1887 by Papus (1865-1916). Today, all of the Martinist orders constitute a living and influential movement carrying the principles and symbols of illuminism.

It will be this last expression of the complex and rich current called "Martinism" that we will go through, in an unusual way for some, in order to identify how Martinism can convey a way of awakening. Beforehand, reading the book *Freemasonry as a Way of Awakening* is recommended, if not necessary. All that has been identified in that essay, to qualify, or to disqualify, Freemasonry as a real initiatory path indeed applies to Martinist orders.

Let us now enter the Martinist Temple.

---

8   In 1778, in Lyon, the national convent of the Gauls of the Strict Observance adopted the reform proposed by Willermoz, which made the Rectified Scottish Rite the heir of the Coën doctrine. The Profession and the Grand Profession, which constitute the secret class of the Rectified Scottish Rite, are charged with preserving the doctrine of the Primitive Cult. In 1782, at the international convention of the Strict Observance, in Wilhelmsbad, Jean-Baptiste Willermoz and his followers adopted the reform of 1778. The Profession and the Grand Profession officially disappeared. Yet this secret class has continued its work in an occult way for two centuries.

Drawing from the 1909 ritual

I The Martinist Ritual

"Just as the sun causes the plants to sprout on the earth's surface and gives life to that which did not have it, so man can animate all that surrounds him and make all the invisible seeds that fill his dark abode bear fruit."

Louis-Claude de Saint-Martin

THE CAREFUL READING, THEN THE STUDY, before its operative implementation, of the Martinist ritual and of a very particular ritual, the one that Robert Ambelain put into use during the Second World War, constitutes a relevant entry into the Martinist world. This ritual synthesizes in a single ceremony the three grades of Associate, Initiate and Unknown Superior who form the traditional framework of Martinist orders.

The ritual, with which Robert Ambelain operated from 1941 to 1952, was intended for *Free Initiates.* We will have to come back to this notion and what it implies in the context of transmission. It was notably used to initiate the members of the Supreme Council of the Martinist Order when Philippe Encausse decided to revive it.[9] It is almost identical to the ritual with which Georges Lagrèze, Jean Chaboseau (son of Augustin Chaboseau, founder of the Tra-

---

9   In 1952, Robert Ambelain used the ritual called "The Initiates of Saint-Martin" to transmit the Martinist initiation to Philippe Encausse and a majority of members of the new Supreme Council of the Martinist Order that Philippe Encausse revived that same year.

ditional Martinist Order in 1931), and Henri Meslin used to initiate Robert Ambelain in December 1940. The story is well-known; we will not reprise it here.

We meet in this ritual the fundamental symbols constitutive of Martinism and the illuminist spirit inherited from Louis-Claude de Saint-Martin. This is not the ritual generally used in Martinist orders that prefer to respect the classical grade scale of Martinism. This ritual is reserved for exceptional situations, but Robert Ambelain, a great operative, whose understanding of ritual was assured, knew how to make it a formidable tool of transmission.

The ritual includes only the degree of Unknown Superior, but it incorporates into its structure the essential elements that make up the two previous degrees of Associate and Initiate (or Associate-Initiate). Robert Ambelain specified in an introduction to the ritual, drafted it seems in 1978, that this degree "can only be conferred on applicants already solidly enriched in matters of esotericism and traditional occultism and already extensively educated," which suggests requirements in both knowledge and praxis.

We shall now discover the text of this ritual, with the exception of the oath that would add nothing more to our study. In bold type, you will find all the words or passages that will be taken up, studied directly, or explained in the twilight mode in the rest of the book, always from a perspective of the way of awakening.

2　Ritual of the Initiates of Saint-Martin[10]

Preparations

The room where the initiation ceremony will take place will be **psychically clean,** the **mirrors will be veiled,** and the **secular luminaries will be extinguished,** with the exception of a single candle on a piece of furniture without any ritual value.

A rectangular table will serve as an altar, oriented in the longest axis of the room, or facing the window, for the best symbolism. It will be covered with a triple layer alternating **the colors black, white and red.** The last will dominate on two thirds of the surface of the table. Before the Initiator will be placed the script, a candelabra with three branches or **three candlesticks** arranged in a triad, the base towards the Initiator, an incense burner or a censer filled with embers, an incense dish, **the Gospel of John open to Chapter 1,** and a sword with a cross guard across the book, the hilt to the Initiator's right.

10　Note again that in the current state of the research there is no ritual filiation going back to Louis-Claude de Saint-Martin in an uninterrupted way, either on the side of the so-called "Papus" filiation or on that of the "Russian" filiation. We can, however, speak of intellectual filiation, of spiritual parentage or, as Robert Amadou liked to recall, of "filiation of desire."

Also to his right will be an empty chair, on which will be placed a white **cloak** of the type used in chivalric orders (the cloak of the CBCS[11] fits the bill perfectly), a black **mask** and a red **cordelier**. On the altar-table, on the operator's right, near the armchair, is a lone candlestick, adorned with a white candle like the others, and a ceremonial mallet.

The Initiator wears a dark cloak or a black robe; he wears the collar of an Unknown Superior and has prepared a similar collar for the candidate, which he keeps near at hand. He can operate in white gloves, except for the ritual frontal transmission. He is masked in black.

The recipient will have fasted for at least six hours, and has abstained from sexual intercourse for at least forty-eight hours. The date of the ceremony will be between the fifth and the tenth day of the waxing moon. The time will be chosen between twenty and twenty-two hours (of the Sun).

The assistants will be arranged in two lines facing each other and will be adorned with the same collar of the Unknown Superior as the Initiator.

Facing the altar, there will be a seat for the candidate.

Ritual

The Initiator gives one knock with the mallet and says:

"Sir (or Madam) I am about to confer on you the traditional initiation according to our Master Louis-Claude de Saint-Martin, such as I received it from my initiator, and such as he himself had received from his, and so on for more than two hundred years. But first I invite you, as I invite my brothers and sisters here, to join with me to **sanctify this room, so that it becomes, by the**

---

11   Knight Beneficent of the Holy City is the ultimate rank of the Rectified Scottish Rite, preceding access to the secret grades of Professed Knight and Grand Professed Knight.

double virtue of speech and gesture, the particular temple in which to celebrate this traditional initiation. That is why, in the form that our Masters once adopted, we enable the Symbols to show themselves."

The Initiator lights the triad of luminaries placed in front of him according to custom, starting with the central candle, then lighting the one to his left, and finally the one on his right. Then he continues:

"**May this one Light, emanating from these several luminaries, reveal to us the mysterious Power of the One who sustains our particular temple, which we are about to raise to the glory of God and of his Son, the Word, Eternal and Uncreated, our Lord. For in the beginning was the Word, and the Word was with God, and the Word was God. All things were made by Him, and without Him was not any thing made that was made. In Him was life, and the life was the Light of men. And the Light shineth in Darkness, and the Darkness comprehendeth it not.**"

The Initiator lights the candle on his right and visualizes the Past Masters of the Order, saying:

"**This is in memory of those who have existed, who are no more, and who exist again, luminous and resplendent.**"

The Initiator pours the incense into the burner in three deposits, then with the right hand (with or without the censer), he traces in space a large Pentagram above and in the scented smoke. He says:

"**Let this incense rise up to Thee, O Lord, as it once was in Thy Holy Temple in Jerusalem, at the hour of the evening sacrifice.**"

After a silence, he continues:

"**Let us gather, my Brothers and Sisters, so that our minds and our hearts may be in union, beyond death, with those of our Brothers of the past.**"

All are silent for a few moments.

The Initiator will pay attention to the various manifestations of the incense burning on the embers. Then he raises his **right hand, thumb squared** and says:

"**Venerated masters who have gone through the Gates and made the last journey, our call will rise to you. With all our Brothers dispersed over the vast world, deign to assemble and unite yourself, at this moment and in this place, with one of yours, in spirit and in heart.**"

The Initiator, after a brief silence, slowly gives three knocks with the mallet. He then raises his right hand wide open, fingers together and thumb squared, and says:

"**Powers of the Kingdom, be under my left foot and in my right hand! Glory and Eternity, touch my two shoulders and lead me in the ways of Victory! Mercy and Justice, be the balance and splendor of my life! Intelligence and Wisdom, give to me the Crown! Spirits of the Kingdom, lead me between the two Columns** that support the entire edifice of the Temple! Angels of Netzach and Hod, strengthen me on the cubic stone of Yesod..."

The Initiator observes a few moments' silence and then resumes:

"**Remember Thy words, O Lord! So Thou saidst: Heaven is My throne and Earth is My footstool. What house will you build for me? What will be the place where I can retire and rest? For all these things exist in them, in the beginning... So you said, O Lord. And I rejoiced in my heart when they said to me: Let us go to the temple of the Lord, to the temple of the Lord God. And behold, my feet stand at thy gates, O heavenly Jerusalem, Jerusalem built as a united city. Peace be in thy walls and safety in thy palaces! For if the Lord builds not the dwelling place, their labor is but lost who build it... Eternal God, Wise and Strong,**

Mighty Being of Beings, be present in this place. Sanctify it by Thy presence and by Thy majesty, so that the purity, chastity, and fullness of Thy Law may reside there. And as the smoke of this incense rises toward Thee, so may Thy virtue and blessing descend on these flagstones. And all of you, Angels and Heavenly Spirits, be present at this consecration! By the Holy, Living and Eternal God, who created you from nothing as well as me, and who at this very moment can plunge me with you all back into nothingness by His sole Wisdom... Amen."

The Initiator is silent for a few moments then resumes:

"Receive, O Lord, according to the wish of the Unknown Philosopher our Master, the homage that Thy servants here present give to Thee in this place. May this mysterious light illuminate our minds and our hearts, as it once glorified the works of our Masters. May these candles illuminate with their living clarity the Brothers gathered at Thy call. May their presence be a living testimony of their union."

Silence.

The Initiator continues:

"In the name of the Word, Eternal and Uncreated, by whom all light and all truth is manifested, I declare this assembly legitimate and valid, united under the auspices of our Master the Unknown Philosopher, in order to perpetuate the mystical influence that he has deposited in us. Let us now evoke the presence of our Master by a statement of the doctrine of the Order he founded.

"In principle, at the root of Being, is the Absolute. **The Absolute, which religions call God, cannot be conceived of, and who claims to define it denatures its notion by assigning limits. But from this unfathomable Absolute emanates eternally the androgynous Dyad formed of two indissolubly united principles: the vivifying Spirit and the universal Living Soul. The mystery of their union constitutes the great mystery of the Word.** Now the Word is the collective Man considered in his divine synthesis, before his disintegration. It is the celestial Adam before the Fall, before this Universal Being had modulated from Unity to Number, from Absolute to Relative, from Collectivity to Individualism, from Infinity to Space, and from Eternity to Time.

"Spurred on by an inner motive about whose essential nature we must be silent, and which we define by a selfish thirst for individual existence, a large number of fragmentary words, potential consciousnesses, vaguely awakened in a mode of emanation from the bosom of the absolute Word, separated from the Word who knows them. They detached themselves, tiny divisions, from the Mother-Unit that had begotten them. Simple rays of this occult Sun, they darted infinitely in the Darkness of their individuality, which they wished to be independent of any previous principle, in a word: autonomous. But as a ray of light has but a relative existence in relation to the focus that produced it, these words, also relative, devoid of the self-sacred principle and of a proper light, darkened as they removed themselves from the absolute Word. They fell into Matter, a lie of Substance into delirium of objectivity, into Matter which is to Non-Being what Spirit is to Being; they descended to elementary existence: to animality, to the vegetable, to the mineral.

"Thus was born the Matter which was immediately elaborated from the Spirit, and the concrete Universe took an ascending life which emerged from the stone, rough from crystallization, to the man capable of thinking, praying, assenting to intelligence, and devoting himself to his fellow men. This sensible repercussion of the captive Spirit, sublimating the progressive forms of Matter and Life in an attempt to escape from its prison, is recognized and studied by contemporary science under the name of evolution. This evolution is the universal redemption of the Spirit. By evolving, the Spirit goes back up. But before going back, it had descended. This is what we call involution. How did the divided word stop at a given point in its fall? What force allowed it to turn back? How did the numbed consciousness of his collective divinity finally awaken in him? There are so many deep mysteries that we can not even address here. Our Order limits its claims to the hope of fertilizing good soil by sowing good seed everywhere. The teachings of the Unknown Superiors are precise, but also elementary. These words and this brief teaching are to be meditated upon at length. They summarize almost the entire program of Saint-Martin known as 'Martinism.' And if our venerable Order can, in its universalism, receive recipients from various religious backgrounds, it is nonetheless obvious that the primary beliefs of these 'Men of Desire' must tend in a general way, not to exacerbate their psychic personality with the prospect of derisory and dangerous powers for their spiritual future, but above all to arm them morally and spiritually for the fight that they will then have to lead against these powers of error and darkness that brought down the Collective Man at the dawn of time.

"And now it is time, Man of Desire, to ask you to take the traditional oath of the Initiates of our Order, which I will read to you and you will then repeat after me, word for word, if you would please stand up and raise your right hand before the Symbols."

It is done. Then the Initiator takes the text signed by the recipient, impales the sheet on the point of the sword **and ignites it in the fire of the candle of the Past Masters.**

The Initiator then says:

"Time alters and erases the word of man, but what is entrusted to Fire endures forever."

He puts the sword down and says:

"Stand, my brothers and sisters. Assist me! I am going, with your assistance and that of our Masters, to transmit the initiation into our Order to this Man of Desire."

The Initiator, or an assistant, places the mask on the recipient's face and says:

"With this mask, **your worldly personality disappears.** You become an unknown, among others equally unknown. You no longer have to fear the petty susceptibilities with which your daily life is constrained, in the midst of a hostile world, constantly trying to find fault. Draw inspiration from the deep symbolism of this ancient, seemingly useless, usage. Finding yourself alone, in front of men you do not know, you have nothing to ask of them, but everything to give them. **Because it is from yourself, from your very isolation, that you will draw the flame to illuminate your inner life...** Unknown, you have no orders or philosophical instructions to receive from anyone in the profane world. Alone, you are responsible for your actions before yourself, before your conscience, that dreaded master to whom you must always look to for advice. For it is he, the inflexible and stern judge, whose mission is to bring you back to your original source.

"This mask will isolate you from the profane world during your work and will also teach you to keep your thoughts secret, your movements secret, and your actions secret. It will remind you of your oath of silence. It is the image of the veil that you will now hold before the occult Light, because you will also have to keep its mystery, which the supreme God has seen fit to conceal.

"Through this mask, realize also how to be an unknown for those whom you will draw from idle ignorance; know how to sanctify your personality whenever you will act as their ignored superior. Thus, you will justify the motto of the Brothers of the Temple: 'Not unto us, O Lord, not unto us, but to Thy name give glory...'"

The Cloak of the Order is placed on the shoulders of the recipient.

The Initiator continues:

"Man of desire, isolated in the study of yourself, it is through your solitary meditation alone that you will succeed in recreating your spiritual personality. So, instead of letting your instincts forge you an illusory, unstable, and even perverse ego, it is your soul alone, this inner god, who will gradually forge it over the coming days. However, beware! The forces of darkness, unleashed against the new elect who is born to the Light, may throw themselves against you. **Learn then how to enfold yourself in the mysterious cloak.** It will render you immune to the attacks of the accomplices of corrupt and inferior Nature."

The cordelier is then looped, under the cloak, around the waist of the recipient.

"Man of desire, by this cordelier, which you will henceforth wear under your cloak, you become a hermit, safe from the evil forces that will besiege you during your work. **The cordelier, symbol of the magic circle and the chain of tradition,** connects you to your Brothers and Sisters, as well as to your Initiator, as it connects these and that one to all those who are no longer, but who tonight, in spirit, are yet there, invisible but present. The cordelier is the image of the chain that connects you to your Brothers and Sisters, the mask is that of secrecy, the cloak of silence and prudence.

"From now on, unknown and solitary traveler, you will continue to traverse the cycle of the present life. You will submit again to the ruling powers of Space and Time. There you will be the messenger of the Word, the docile agent of the First Cause, the Sower of Truth, in spiritual communion with all your Brothers and Sisters, with the living and with the dead.

"On your way, sowing seeds of light and wisdom, you will continue the initiatory journey. Whenever you see a chance or necessity imposes it, you will knock on a new door. Wherever the star of the Magi shines, you will recognize a new stage.

You will seek Knowledge there, and you will seek it everywhere: within the starry firmament, in the evocative symbolism of the constellations, in the yellowed parchments, in the reddening of the athanors, as in the arches of the sacred monuments. But you will only encounter Wisdom in the depths of your inner temple, where, according to the promise, in the darkness of the sanctuary, God sometimes speaks to Israel!

"And on every anniversary of this day, **scrutinizing your memories behind the iconic mask,** you will find that your knowledge will have grown. Thus, in your immediate sphere, you will have worked, sometimes unconsciously and without perceiving it, to build a better universe, just as you will have created the seed of the future god in yourself. May you then justify this prophetic word: 'Those who have possessed the divine knowledge will shine with all the light of Heaven, but those who have transmitted it to men according to the ways of justice, will shine like stars in all eternity...'"

The Initiator then places himself in front of the recipient, makes him kneel, disengages his right hand, places it on the top of the candidate's head, and pronounces the formula of investiture:

"I, X (Order name), regularly initiated by Y (Order name of his own initiator), in the Name of God Almighty and Eternal, by virtue of the powers that I have received, **I create you, receive you, and constitute you an Unknown Superior** of our Order, according to the teaching of Louis-Claude de Saint-Martin, with his permission, by his order, and under his auspices. Rise up my Brother (or my Sister)."

The Initiator then takes the right hand of the new Brother (or the new Sister) and raises it in front of the candle of the Past Masters.

"Brothers, I present to you X (Order name of the new Un-

known Superior), Unknown Superior of our Order, and I ask you
to accept him (or her) among us."

There is silence, and we observe the possible manifestations in
the flame of the candle of the Past Masters.

The Initiator continues:

"My Brothers and Sisters, **please remove from the new member of our Order the three symbols we have just put on him (or her).**"

It is done. The Initiator resumes:

"My Brother (my Sister) receive **the white collar of the Unknown Superiors of our Order and its age-old Pantacle.** Wear
them to victory! May they be to you henceforth like the protective
shield of your chest, and before them may the evil powers hostile
to man be effaced and disappear."

Silence.

Initiator:

"My Brothers and Sisters, let us form the fraternal chain, in
spiritual union with our Brothers of times passed."

All form the chain. The Initiator then recites Psalm CXXXIII:

"Behold, how good and how pleasant it is for brethren to
dwell together in unity! It is like the precious ointment upon the
head, that ran down upon the beard, even Aaron's beard: that
went down to the skirts of his garments; as the dew of Hermon,
and as the dew that descended upon the mountains of Zion: for
there the Lord commanded the blessing, even life for evermore...
Amen."

All repeat: "Amen."

Initiator:

"Brothers and sisters, let us break the chain and resume our
places."

The Initiator then states the formula for closing the work:

"May Peace, Joy, and Charity be in our hearts and on our lips, now and until the day of our terrestrial death. Angels and Spirits who have assisted us, may the peace of God be forever between you and us, as you return to your blessed abodes."

He extinguishes with the snuffer or with his fingers the candle of the past Masters, then the lights of the altar, in the reverse order of their lighting: the candle on the right, that on the left, then that in the center.

Initiator:

"My brothers and sisters, the work is closed. Let us withdraw in peace."

3   Martinist Propositions

"Why are we immortal? It is that we descend from the essence
and faculties of God, and that a living and eternal being cannot
produce perishable beings.
"Why are we not God as the same unity? It is because we are
detached from God while His faculties are not and cannot be,
because they are God like Him."

Louis-Claude de Saint-Martin

BEFORE EXAMINING FURTHER the ritual called the *Initiates of
Saint-Martin,* it is useful to take an interest in the work of the
Unknown Philosopher, which remains the general framework in
which the Martinist rituals, operations, and orders are inscribed.

Here is an essay on weaving Martinism from the key ideas
identified by Louis-Claude de Saint-Martin and developed in his
writings. To go further it is necessary, it is essential to study the
remarkable prefaces and presentations of the books of Louis-
Claude de Saint-Martin written by Robert Amadou for the edition of the complete works of the Unknown Philosopher issued
by the publisher Georg Olms.

Louis-Claude de Saint-Martin[12]

Rather than producing a catalog of quotations, it seemed more useful to identify the ideas that constitute the vectors of the thought of the Unknown Philosopher, living thought that was nourished by spiritual experience and the encounter with other works of great seekers, from Emmanuel Swedenborg to Jacob Bœhme. We find traces of this evolution in the succession of the writings of Louis-Claude de Saint-Martin. We indicate, for each of the ideas presented below, the source, or one of the possible sources, in the writings of the Unknown Philosopher, so that the reader can easily turn to the work dealing with the subject mentioned.

12   Based on an 1847 engraving by Adolphe Gusman (1821-1905) for the review *Le Magasin pittoresque* edited by Edouard Charton. It would have been executed from a portrait made around 1780. For other portraits of the Unknown Philosopher, see the excellent website: www.philosophe-inconnu.com and the special issue of *La Tour Saint Jacques,* 3rd quarter 1961, dedicated to Louis-Claude de Saint-Martin.

- Only the True Philosopher, Unknown in fact, that is to say, not acting as a "person," but as a free being, unmasked and yet without a face, has access to the Truth. All others wander in the errors of the re-presentation, be it encyclopedic, philosophical, religious, scientific, or even supposedly initiatory. (*Des erreurs et de la Vérité*)

- God, Christ, and me. Reintegration: me in Christ, Christ in God, me in God, God in me. The One. (*Des erreurs et de la Vérité*)

- There can be no Reintegration without the grace of Sophia. (*Des erreurs et de la Vérité*)

- Man is the point of consciousness of the Divine in the darkness of creation. (*Des erreurs et de la Vérité*)

- The material is not true. It is necessary to go through it in order to grasp the Real. (*Des erreurs et de la Vérité*)

- There is a chain of correspondences that allows you to climb or lose yourself. Enlightened consciousness or darkened consciousness. This multidimensional mesh constitutes the creation. (*Des erreurs et de la Vérité*)

- The human being is the bearer of choice. His free will directs creation towards the light or towards the darkness. (*Des erreurs et de la Vérité*)

- Initiation is opposed to the multiple. Simplification tends, even introduces, to the One. Truth meets in the center. Every mistake is an off-center aspect of Truth. Truth is non-human, in other words, the unconditional. (*Des erreurs et de la Vérité*)

- Truth and its variations are accessible and perceptible only in the Silence and the Secret. They relate to the unspeakable and the ineffable. (*Des erreurs et de la Vérité*)

- Beauty requires secrecy and exclusivity. Those who do not know how to "see" can not be invited to "see." (*Des erreurs et de la Vérité*)

- Formulations are futile. Language traps consciousness. It is the contemplation of the essence within that lifts the veil. (*Des erreurs et de la Vérité*)

- Man is the very sign of God. He proves it by deifying not only himself, but the whole. A man of desire, he leaves room for the Spirit in order to become the New Man, the only one empowered to ensure the ministry of the spirit-man for the benefit of all beings. (*Tableau naturel des rapports qui existent entre Dieu, l'homme et l'univers*)

- The Great Work has a double aspect, internal then external in appearance, internal and external in reality. (*Tableau naturel des rapports qui existent entre Dieu, l'homme et l'univers*)

- In Silence, the free and absolute Will of Being calls upon the Word to fill us. Without Silence, there is no Word. Without the Word, there is no return to the One. (*Tableau naturel des rapports qui existent entre Dieu, l'homme et l'univers*)

- The fire of desire nourishes our imitation of the center of everything. Desire, which is built on and through otherness, becomes will when one reaches the center and imitation becomes pure creation. (*Tableau naturel des rapports qui existent entre Dieu, l'homme et l'univers*)

- The internal is the direct path to reintegration, a path without a symbol and without a signature. Theosophy is only internal. (*Tableau naturel des rapports qui existent entre Dieu, l'homme et l'univers*)

- Initiation is addressed to the man of desire, the man who wants to leave the stream out of desire for God and who recognizes himself as the desire of God, who is desire for freedom. The initiate is a free man, free of himself. (*L'Homme de désir*)

- God is the principle of man. Man is the hand, the heart, and the eye of God. His mirror too. (*L'Homme de désir*)

- Desire is opposed to envy. It is a vertical, ascending desire, a magical power, the only one, which aims to extract itself from the illusory world, radically. Initiation is therefore an abandonment. (*L'Homme de désir*)

- Initiation passes from the suffering Christ to the glorious Christ. (*Ecce homo*)

- Man is the means of God. He is posterior to Him only in temporality. In the center, outside of time, the means and the principle are One. (*Ecce homo*)

- Man is the means between his original nature, divine, and his ultimate nature, divine. (*Ecce homo*)

- Anything that does not lead to the center, all that does not awaken, maintains the prison of representations. So many identifications, so many demons. (*Ecce homo*)

- God calls us to the center. The demons are therefore peripheral. (*Ecce homo*)

- To stop on the way to the center is to take the risk of identifying with a partial truth that will quickly decay into error and confusion. (*Ecce homo*)

- The New Man is new because he is older than the old one. The erasure of the old man is the original man asserting himself. (*Le Nouvel Homme*)

- The New Man, of whom Christ is the model—but we are no longer in imitation—freed from the conditioning of the body and the psyche, lives through the spirit. (*Le Nouvel Homme*)

- The New Man is generated, or re-generated, by the return of desire to the center of everything and by his arising at the same time as his election. This is the very condition for reintegration. (*Le Nouvel Homme*)

- The New Man, thought of God, means of God, is also His Word, His Will, His Celebration, His Theurgy. The ceremonial theurgy which invokes, requiring the co-operation of all the powers and emanations, prepares the internal theurgy in the same hierarchy of spirits. (*Le Nouvel Homme*)

- God, the Christ, the angels, the "good companion," all are in him, the New Man, and all are through him. (*Le Nouvel Homme*)

- Angels cooperate. It is Man who is the key. (*Le Nouvel Homme*)

- God, Christ, Holy Spirit. But also Sophia, inseparable from God. (*Le Nouvel Homme*)

- The original nature of man is androgynous. It is Sophia who restores this androgyny by a renewed marriage with the soul when the New Man recovers his divine nature. (*Le Nouvel Homme*)

- If by union with the spirit of Christ we let the numbers live in us, then the Great Work proceeds in perfection. (*Le Nouvel Homme*)

- Man is a mediator between good and evil, and also a battleground for both. Truth and Sophia help him so that in him and through him the good prevails. (*Le Nouvel Homme*)

- Silence, thought, word, operation, such is the unfolding of the action of the Holy Spirit. (*Le Nouvel Homme*)

- The kaleidoscope of our spiritual life must ultimately give only one image, that of universal unity. (*Le Nouvel Homme*)

- Through the invisible baptism, the second baptism, divine, no longer human, the New Man—body, soul and spirit—becomes the receptacle of the divine word, and the seven ways of the Spirit open in him as well as the twelve gifts that had slept in his being until then. (*Le Nouvel Homme* and *Le Ministère de l'homme-esprit*)

- Through analogical knowledge and transmutational power, the New Man performs a triple resurrection (body, soul, and spirit) and regenerates himself in the divine life and with him all that is. The New Man is also a new healer. (*Le Nouvel Homme* and *Le Ministère de l'homme-esprit*)

- The separate tradition of the law is no more than an obscurity. The New Man discerns the law behind the tradition and revives the tradition by the law, the law of the Spirit. (*Le Nouvel Homme*)

- It is not by form, but by fire, that the New Man operates. (*Le Nouvel Homme*)

- The spirit goes to the spirit. The ineffable goes to the ineffable. It is man who must take the first step. (*Le Nouvel Homme*)

- The New Man is the point in the center of the hexagram, a point of perfect balance between the divine ternary and the spiritual ternary, the place of exercise of the Ministry of the spirit-man. (*Le Nouvel Homme* and *Le Ministère de l'homme-esprit*)

- The New Man knows in his heart that the whole history of Christ unfolds in his flesh in a transfiguration, a true rebirth, which not only makes him leave the prison of the world, but transforms this prison into a higher chamber. (*Le Nouvel Homme* and *Le Ministère de l'homme-esprit*)

- He who consoles is also the one who liberates. (*Le Nouvel Homme*)

- It is through internal alchemy that spiritual substances are extracted from heavy corporeality. This voluntary death before death is the door that allows the exit from the tomb. (*Le Nouvel Homme*)

- The New Man, in his glorious body, reigns less through powers than through love. (*Le Nouvel Homme*)

- The New Man grasps and seizes the Spirit of Things to exercise the Ministry of the spirit-man. (*De l'esprit des choses* and *Le Ministère de l'homme-esprit*)

- Knowledge is active in the movement of the mind to seek itself in the things it generates by "magical imagination." (*De l'esprit des choses*)

- Earth—body—soul—spirit—God, a range that plays with reflections. A play of mirrors, material, spiritual, divine, to the highest of the Heavens. Knowing how to read the diffractions of light right down to nature allows us to remain in verticality. (*De l'esprit des choses*)

- The New Man is a point in Sophia's mirror without which God cannot think or contemplate Himself, con-template or imagine. To imagine is to engender. (*De l'esprit des choses*)

- Do not get lost in names. The more you name, the less you are. The more you name, the less you perceive the root numbers and ineffable letters of things. (*De l'esprit des choses*)

- The way is first negative. You have to decide: give up, give up. Neither this nor that. In silence, it is then the being who calls the divine true, the divine beautiful, the divine good. This divine responds with Gnosis and the beatitudes. (*Le Nouvel Homme* and *De l'esprit des choses*)

The simple reader, let alone the student of the Saint-Martinist work, immediately grasps that we are not in the presence of a religious dogma or a confused doctrine, but a profound teaching born of the strong experience of Being. Louis-Claude de Saint-Martin will have inscribed this founding experience in the language that was his, a language that remains very accessible to us. The occultists of the late nineteenth and early twentieth century, Papus and Stanislas de Guaita, at the head of the Companions of Hierophany, have translated the heritage of Saint-Martin into another language, that of their time still marked by the romantic influence and that of the ritual with its very particular poetry.

Today, without betraying these two legitimate expressions, it is possible to extract the essence of what comprises the Martinist way, often described as the way of the heart and as a way of awakening, to express it in a more current language.

4   Saint-Martin, Nondualist

EVERY AUTHENTIC INITIATIC TRADITION is essentially nondual, although its temporal expression may be presented under a dualistic modality, whether this is due to the Aristotelian structure of language or because of its distance from the source. The traditions of ancient Egypt are nondual: Isis is the equal of Re; it is the Greeks and especially Plutarch who by ignorance or strategy created a dualistic reading of it. Greek dualism influenced Christian movements leading to the dualistic tension of the Church of Rome, while esoteric Christianity remained oriented towards nondualism.

The doctrine of reintegration of Martines de Pasqually, inscribed by Jean-Baptiste Willermoz in the Rectified Scottish Rite and internalized by Louis-Claude de Saint-Martin, may at first glance appear dualistic with its two falls and its great exorcisms. However, the very idea of reintegration is fundamentally nondual and inclusive of all that comes through an operative annulment of all separation.

The distinction made by Louis-Claude de Saint-Martin—man of the stream, man of desire, new man, man-spirit—describes an initiatory process that goes from the dualistic division of the stream to the absolute unity and freedom of the Spirit—duality, nonduality in duality, nonduality, neither duality nor nonduality—from confinement in duality to the absolute freedom of the Lord.

A prayer by Louis-Claude de Saint-Martin, stunning in both its form and its operative dimension, perfectly expresses the non-dual dimension, the final impossibility of separation from God. It is interesting that it is characterized as "theurgic." Indeed, it is not a classic invocation of reintegration. It takes note of what is and what remains of the identity of man and of God (whatever the state of the latter), to re-establish Being consciously within its own nature, by a reversal as audacious as it is effective.

In these few words, we have the essence of the direct way of Saint-Martin.

Theurgic prayer
Louis-Claude de Saint-Martin

UNIVERSAL BEING, BEHOLD the state where sin has put you within me; have mercy on yourself, sympathize with your own fate, lay claim to yourself against the usurpers, keep your word to yourself, that the sacred will not countenance corruption. Who would dare to dispute your rights, if you but made the gesture of claiming them?

Unite without a moment's delay to all that you have sown in the different regions of your being, to all these treasures that belong to you by an irrefutable title, since they are nothing but yourself; fly to your own help, for there is no portion of me that does not put you in danger, as well as exposing you to the most shameful advances and most frightful torments.

A single groan, a cry, or a threat will suffice for everything to return to order and for life to be no longer separated from life. You show generosity to preserve my joys; how could I not show tenderness to take care of your pains! You want me to live, and I would not think of preventing you from dying!

It is not for myself that I want to pray to you. I only want you to pray for you, I want to reciprocate what you do without ceasing for men; for it is for them and not for you that you take care of them.

Fonds Z, Chauvin file, A2, room 13; autograph
Discovered by Robert Amadou
Posted in *L'Esprit des Choses* (CSM XVII)

5   Ritual Commentary

"The universe is both full of evidence and incredulous."
Louis-Claude de Saint-Martin

LET US SPECIFY ONCE AGAIN that it is not a question here of carrying out a hermetic or illuminist exegesis of the ritual and its symbolism. It is enough for the reader to refer to the works of the Unknown Philosopher and to the remarkable works of certain seekers. This commentary intends to demonstrate in what way Martinism, today as in its beginnings, is an excellent vehicle for the philosophies and praxis of awakening and thus to remind that the Martinist orders have a particular responsibility in this domain.

The initiatory function

The initiatory orders have the function, indeed the mission, of preparing seekers for the Great Adventure, the quest for the Absolute, the Real, Liberation, Awakening, the Self, the Ultimate Experience, the final Reintegration according to the doctrine of the Order of Knight Masons Elus Coëns of the Universe, inscribed internally in Martinism. Whatever expression is chosen to signify the liberation from all limits and conditions, the experience of one's own permanence is transcendent.

We have already stated elsewhere[13] how initiation can be analyzed:

On the ways of Awakening, we distinguish four relationships to the Real. If the quester immediately grasps that he is the Absolute, the quest is completed, here and now, forever; it never began. Everything is accomplished.

If he does not grasp the Absolute, but perceives the play of Consciousness and Energy, he plays instead of being played.

If the quester remains foreign to the game of Consciousness and Energy, then he celebrates and respects the rites.

If he does not understand the meaning of the rites, he puts himself at the service of others and serves his neighbor.

"The key to initiation, the Line of Silence, which must be crossed by an abandonment, a leap into the void, is located in this doorless passage between rites and divine play, from imitation to invention, in this 'quantum' leap between the dual and the nondual.

This tetrad, altruism—rites—game of Consciousness and Energy—Absolute, can be expressed in other terms. Thus: form—symbol—method—Awakening or, in the field of therapy: medicine and surgery—spagyric and herbal medicine—alchemy and energetic therapy—Awakening which is the ultimate cure. Finally, more provocatively, the stupidity[14] that is believing that one understands and acts, idiocy; the antidote to stupidity which consists in not understanding anything, blocking thought, the prelude to silence; then controlled madness; and finally Awakening.

---

13 *Le Discours de Venise* by Rémi Boyer (Cordes-sur-Ciel, Fr: Rafael de Surtis, 2007).

14 An expression of what Gilles Deleuze defines as "the digestive and leguminous fund" of the human.

All initiatory science, all initiatory art, therefore strives to lead the candidate into this Silence, a true Immaculate Conception, the only obligatory passage that everyone must discover and attain to rend the veil of forms. This is because, the ritual tells us, "The Absolute, which religions call God, cannot be conceived of, and he who claims to define it distorts the notion by assigning limits to it." It is outside of language, outside of concept, that the Absolute can live and know everything while remaining unspeakable. It is outside of language that the human being can get closer to himself, to his true original and ultimate nature because, as has been well practiced and taught by Serge Célibidache, the great conductor (in a field very close to initiation, that of music), when we grasp that the beginning and the end are identical, everything is perfect.

The human being must still the world of representations, concepts, and language and enter the Silence in order to perceive the world instead of conceiving and conceptualizing it, to reach the objective state that differentiates the living from the one who is lived, the rude accident resulting from conditioning.

The Line of Silence is an experience that makes us abandon the multiple and the complex for the One and the Simple, leaving the dualistic illusion for the nondual reality.

> On either side of the Line of Silence, two different worlds stand out: the One and the Other, two experiences of the Real, the one not true, illusory and ephemeral, apparently external and temporal, the other true, immutable and eternal, better, 'internal.' The true and the not-true are nonetheless the same.
>
> In the One, there is Being. In the Other, the person.
>
> In the One, we are in the objective state, the pure perception of what is there. Universe perceived. In the Other, we remain in a

subjective state. Universe thought, conceived.[15]

In the One, we are inscribed in the non-time of the here and now. In the Other, we are in time.

In the One, we are the devourers of time, past, present, and future. In the Other, we are the prey of time.

In the One, we are alive. In the Other, we are lived.

In the One, we are in Silence. In the Other, we are in the midst of noise and language.[16]

In the One, the Word is creator. In the Other, the utterance is lost.

In the One, all is freedom. In the Other, there are only conditions and limits.

In the One, the body is Spirit. In the Other, the body is matter.

In the One, all poison becomes liquor of the gods. In the Other, everything is toxic.

In the One, all is perfect stillness and fluidity. In the Other, everything is movement and heaviness.

In the One, all is love. In the Other, all is desire.

In the One, all is the fullness of the void. In the Other, everything is empty, despairing of forms.

In the One is the formless. In the Other, are the forms.

In the One, we are in the invention. In the Other, we are in the imitation.

In the Other, the power—territory—reproduction triangle[17] acts fully in all the peripheries of the experience. In the One, this same triangle is verticalized in a single point of Void.

15   According to Spinoza, we can experience and feel our eternity but we cannot think it. The experience of eternity is for Spinoza an experience of intensity, which is opposed to that of extension, an intensity of which everyone has had, at least once, the intuition.

16   See *Mysterium Magnum* by Jacob Bœhme (Paris: Aubier, 1945), the passage devoted to the word and the sensory language, pp. 456-457.

17   The power—territory—reproduction triangle is the basis of the existent and the opposition between existents, whether they are minerals, plants, animals, or humans, who want to appropriate parts considered as external.

Initiation, which remains a counterculture, is a process that repels and dissolves the "person" in the light of Being. The individual, the indivisible part of each, which some will call divine, this part of the Real which persists under the magma of the peripheries of the representation can reconquer the place which is his, that is to say the whole place, the All.

"But from this unfathomable Absolute emanates eternally the androgynous Dyad formed of two indissolubly united principles: the vivifying Spirit and the universal living Soul. The mystery of their union constitutes the great mystery of the Word," says the ritual. If language is unfit to comprehend the Real, in the zone of Silence, from the union of two principles, Spirit and Soul, Pneuma and Soma, is born the Word. The Word is the creator. There is a collapse of the Word, from its origin within Silence, in its extension as speech in temporality and its exhaustion in language until it merges with noise. Unlike language, which dilutes consciousness in dreams, the Word accompanies the increased awareness of what Is. That is why Tradition insists on the power of Silence, superior to the power of the Word. Without Silence, the Word is only verbiage and noise. Let us remember the famous maxim of the Unknown Philosopher: "I wanted to do good, but I did not want to make noise because I felt that the noise was not good and the good was not noisy." The Unknown Superior is an Unknown Silent.

We can illustrate the initiatory process with a diagram. If "The map is not the territory,"[18] the map can help the traveler to know in what part of the territory he is and how to orient himself, knowing that the initiatory Orient is always "in a Higher Sense" as taught by François Rabelais.

---

18 First axiom of the General Semantics of Alfred Korzybski.

ABSOLUTE
THE GREAT REAL
FREE SPIRIT
GOD

World of Essence
Neither dual nor nondual

The Absolute	*Beingness*
Spirit	*Soul*
Pneuma	*Soma*

World of Consciousness-Energy
Nonduality

SILENCE
Objective state
Being
Timelessness
Motionlessness
The Internal
The Word

World of Form
The person — The mask
Subject — object duality
Having and Doing
Temporality — Language — Speech — Concept — Movement
Subjective state
Existence
Power — Territory — Reproduction

Preliminaries and prerequisites

Three excerpts from the ritual give us indications of the prerequisites or pre-qualifications necessary to approach the sacred:

"The room where the initiation ceremony will take place will be psychically clean, the mirrors will be veiled, and the secular luminaries will be extinguished..."

It is advisable to "sanctify this room, so that it becomes, by the double virtue of speech and gesture, the particular temple in which to celebrate this traditional initiation."

"The recipient will have fasted for at least six hours, and will have abstained from sexual intercourse for at least forty-eight hours..."

These excerpts put into perspective the question of the profane person and the sacred person on the one hand and of mastery on the other.

Every initiation ceremony creates a sacred "person" and a profane "person," a sacred time and a profane time. This artifice within the representation of the world has the function of weakening the egotistical force by dividing it and constituting the first witness, that is to say, the one who observes the play of the two persons, sacred and profane, within the conditioned person, the passage from one time to another.

We will not come back to this play, which is essential to know well in order to identify the dysfunctions that are sure to appear and to create the conditions conducive to initiation.

Let us simply recall that the *Theory of Three Persons*[19] reveals a series of dysfunctions that should be identified:

---

19 *Freemasonry as a Way of Awakening* by Rémi Boyer (Bayonne, NJ: Rose Circle, 2020).

- Dysfunctions in the group, obedience, or order.
- Dysfunctions in one or the other person:
  ○ Dysfunctions within the profane person;
  ○ Irruption of the profane person within the sacred person;
  ○ Invasion of the sacred person by the profane person;
  ○ Cannibalization of the profane person by the sacred person.
- Dysfunctions of the witness.

"The mirrors will be veiled." This is a very beautiful metaphor to signify that consciousness is no longer reflected in the reflections of itself through the play of identifications. Wherever I look, I cannot see my image and thus reinforce the "egoic" game. I do not project myself. I do not study myself as subject. I do not contemplate myself in a narcissistic posture. By self-remembering, I settle myself in a "here and now" from which the past and future are excluded, a place-state in which the "person" does not meet his own image in order to feed on it and so nourish it in a morbid entropy. Note that the mirrors are veiled, but they still exist. I am not yet free from attachment to the ego, the mask, the "person," but I know to escape from its toxic influence within the enveloping and benevolent parenthesis of sacred time.

"The secular luminaries will be extinguished." Just as the Freemason leaves his metals at the door of the Temple, the Martinist initiate enters the sacred enclosure without the profane knowledge that guides him in his daily experience. The criteria, the values, the beliefs, most often unconscious, which determine his behavioral, emotional, and intellectual choices in the world of having and doing, are neutralized in order to let the singular light of Being illuminate the field of his consciousness cleansed of all "worldliness," of all impurity. "Psychically clean" means without thought. From the initiatory point of view, all thought is impure since it comes to veil or tarnish the immaculate consciousness of Being.

Then, in this zone of Silence, speech and gesture will be virtuous, free of all intention, all desire, all need. Speech will be creative, gesture will emphasize beauty. Both will only be a celebration of what remains. The particular temple where the traditional initiation is celebrated is none other than this zone of Silence, the Middle Chamber of the Master Mason.

The ritual evokes the three masteries. The candidate for initiation must be fasting and have abstained from sexual intercourse. There is no mention in this ritual of a third condition which generally accompanies the previous two, a condition still in use in somewhat serious orders of chivalry, but which unfortunately is lost, that of the vigil. Through this triple requirement, not very demanding, it is the first mastery that is indicated, that of the gross, saturnine body, without which one cannot control the emotional, lunar body, and the mental, mercurial body. Eliphas Levi, whose influence on Papus and the Companions of Hierophany is known, insisted on abstinence. "Knowing how to use and not to use is to be able to use twice." Whoever wants to advance on the path, to free himself from the conditioning of the person, will one day have to enter asceticism, overcome hunger by prolonged fasting, overcome the archaic command by sexual abstinence, and finally, overcome sleep by vigilance, a vigil of prayer or meditation. It is then no longer a matter of a few hours, but a few weeks for food, a few months or more for sexual abstinence, and a few days for the vigil, until the archaic brain submits to the call of verticality.

After these asceticisms, the man of desire, whose desire is thus verticalized, can eat according to his choices, have a restless sex life if he wishes, and sleep his fill. He can use and not use. He thus masters the powerful calls of the physical body. He can resume asceticism when he wishes, or plunge into the delights of matter without becoming its slave.

Self-remembering, mastery of archaic forces, silence: here in a few words are the prerequisites for initiation. Ritual initiation is thus a preparation, a re-orientation, a break in the conditioning of the "person" in order to bestow the intuition of Being, of the Self, of the Real, of God. There is no real initiation in the generally accepted sense, nor any transmission (another perverted concept, since the "person," the "me," is not only not initiatable, but constitutes the obstacle, while the Self, the Real, "That which remains," has no need of initiation). Initiation is a technical breach in representation, a shock, and transmission is not the reception of any deposit, but a crossing, a leap into the Void and the Fullness of Being. It is only our conceptual alienation, our hypertrophied need for concepts, our identification with temporal linearity and the cause-effect that dress in formalism and obsolete formalities that which is infinite, inexpressible, and permanent.

Of the temporary and the timeless

The notion of initiatory Lineage is very significant in traditional currents, in the East, Far or Middle, as in the West, Christian or not.

Martinism expresses it through the notion of Past Masters: "This is in memory of those who have existed, who are no more, and who exist again, luminous and resplendent," the ritual says, pointing to the candle of the Past Masters.

We will distinguish the notion of temporal lineage, itself double, from the notion of vertical lineage.

By referring to the Past Masters, the Martinist ritual appeals to the traditional notion of lineage and transmission of an initiatory deposit. The word "Tradition," etymologically, refers to the notion of transmission, but Tradition, in all its forms, concludes that we can only be initiated by ourselves and thereby understand our own reality. Transmission has meaning only in the representation and not in the Real as we suggested previously. The transmission is multi-historical. There is no history, but rather histories, temporal and structured by language and culture, in which or through which Tradition expresses itself and is received, passing through the filters and perceptual biases of people. It resides in a more or less coherent set of founding myths, symbols generating meaning constituting a sacred language, and techniques that contribute to a traditional operativity,[20] whether it is divinatory, magical, theurgic or alchemical. All this is born, lives, transforms, and dies in the world of form. All this evokes, sometimes invokes, an elsewhere, the world of consciousness-energy, then the world of essence, worlds that are to be conquered, or explored, or manifested, depending on one's belief system. The primary function of transmission, which occurs often—but not only—through ritual initiation, is to transform the man or woman of the stream into a man or a woman of desire, and then to give them the weapons and tools necessary for the accomplishment of the New Man, to train them in order to make them skilled in the handling of these tools. Let us note that these tools, these weapons and the techniques that accompany them, are transmitted to the "sacred person" under the watchful eye of the witness who is the guarantor of the proper use of these vectors of change.

Formal initiation and transmission thus create a new paradigm favorable to initiation into the Real, into the conscious experience of the Self.

The temporal lineage conveys the conditions of initiation and not the initiation itself.

This temporal lineage, spiritual or "occult" or "initiatory," is most often distinguished from the ancestral and biological lineage, even if they can sometimes still coincide. The ancestral

---

20 [Trans.] Operativity (French, *opérativité*): in this context, a way of work with an internal or esoteric component (e.g., alchemy, divination, ritual, etc.).

lineage manifests the archaic triangle of the species: power—territory—reproduction. It can be effectively called together with the spiritual lineage to deal with changes in the field of representation. Traditional therapies that know how to call upon ancestral energy come particularly to mind.

The vertical lineage, on the contrary, refers to the exit from the peripheries of having and doing, the abandonment of representations, concepts, and beliefs, the grasp of the axis of the Real, the immutable center. We could say that the temporal lineage, in its double aspect, leads to the vertical lineage into which it must disappear with the dissolution of time.[21] Initiation is an "alignment" with oneself. The Past Masters are those who, by renouncing time and ego, have manifested this verticality which makes them "luminous and alive." The man and woman inscribed in the stream, and even in the desire for verticality, are lived rather than alive, lived by their conditioning, dark rather than luminous, obscured by the veil of concepts. They live again, not as a "person," not as an "ego," but as unidentified, unseparated Being, free of all form and capable of all forms simultaneously. The Self.

Moreover, the ritual refers to the flame of the Past Masters, more than to the personalities of the Past Masters. It is remarkable that the initiator has the oath taken by the petitioner signed, then "impales the sheet on the point of the sword and ignites it in the fire of the candle of the Past Masters." The trace of the oath, that is, the bond, temporality, history, is given to the fire. The form is consumed. Only the spirit remains. The flame of the Past Masters is indeed that force of the destruction of forms and times that breaks all ties, liberates the Self, and allows its radiance.

21 The hypertrophy of the feeling of historical filiation, which characterizes the Masonic and esoteric environment of our time, is born of the absence of initiatory axis. Many "initiates" simply frequent traditions without practicing them. They therefore exalt the needs for recognition and belonging to the detriment of satisfying the need for realization.

This is by no means a reference to a hypothetical survival after death as an ego or as a person, or an allusion to reincarnation.

Both post-mortem survival and reincarnation are exoteric doctrines, with educational and therapeutic uses, even social and political ones, conceptualized by the ego that does not accept its own disappearance. Our reality, which was never born, cannot die. Only the fear of the "me" in the face of nothingness justifies all these very contradictory doctrines that have meaning only within the concept of time, which we know to be illusory.

Recall that Louis-Claude de Saint-Martin is not a reincarnationist, that Martines de Pasqually does not mention it, that Emmanuel Swedenborg considers reincarnation as a disease of the soul. The doctrine of reincarnation developed within the Martinist Order after the Theosophical Society had popularized it in esoteric circles.

From an illuminist point of view, the challenge is to become another Christ, in this body, in this life, and not to dwell on supposed past or future incarnations, which are just additional forms to be crossed to reach one's own intrinsic reality, just more ways for the ego to flee the "judgment" of the Real, a judgment that inevitably makes it disappear.

The manifestation of the three lineages, ancestral, spiritual, and vertical, is represented in the "emblematic figure of the universe" that we are going to explore now. This figure, which we somewhat reductively call a hexagram, symbolizes the function and action of the three lineages. The archaic energy of the ancestral lineage represented by the lower triangle is straightened and rectified by the action of the spiritual lineage, the upper triangle, in the field of temporality, the circle, in order to determine a middle chamber, the zone of Silence, the hexagon, whose central point symbolizes both the vertical lineage and the point of Void, the interval, door to the Great Real.

Triangulations

Martinism is marked by the number three: three degrees, three colors (black, white, and red, which refer to the steps of the alchemical Great Work), three candles, three fundamental symbols. The triangle, alone or entwined with its inverted reflection to create a hexagram, is intended to summarize all Martinism. It is these "few points" that are the basis of the Martinist initiation, structured by the number three, and which invite us to take an interest in the famous Martinist seal, often referred to, since Papus, by the expression "Martinist pantacle."[22] Here is the drawing, by the hand of Louis-Claude de Saint-Martin himself.

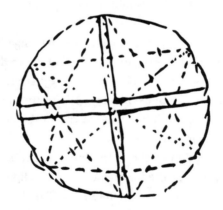

---

22 The word "pantacle" comes from the Greek *panta*, "all." It designates any geometric figure that is meant to model a universal, formal, energetic, or absolute structure. The word should not be confused with "pentacle," from the Greek *pente*, "five," which designates the five-pointed star, symbol of the accomplished man.

The "Martinist pantacle" comes from Louis-Claude de Saint-Martin. He calls it the "emblematic figure of the universe." He gives an initial explanation in the treatise *Les Nombres*[23] and presents its function: "Independently of the numerical proofs we find in the theosophical addition of 3 and 4 to make sure that 4 is a central number and 3 a circumferential number, the geometric laws provide us with very convincing proofs to distinguish our origin from that of matter, to show us our superiority over all physical nature, our direct relations with our principle and the immortal duration of our being which drew life from immortality itself."

The function of the seal is to help us to grasp our original nature and to draw the outline of what constitutes a path of immortality, not of immortality to last, but of an "internality" concomitant with Awakening.

Louis-Claude de Saint-Martin calls for geometry. We all know the importance of sacred geometries in the world of initiation, be it the geometry of builders, the geometry of wisdom, or the secret geometry of intervals. Obviously, Louis-Claude de Saint-Martin was a Geometer if we refer to his presentation:

All of these truths are found written in the circle naturally divided into six parts. The natural circle was formed differently from the artificial circle of geometers. The center called for the upper triangle and the lower triangle which, reacting mutually, manifested life. It was then that the quaternary man appeared. It would be quite impossible to find this quaternary in the circle without employing wasted and superfluous lines, if we were limited to the method of the geometers. Nature loses nothing; she coordinates all parts of her works, each for each. Also, in the circle regularly

---

23 Autograph manuscript belonging to *Fonds Z*, deposited at the Municipal Library of Lyon, the transcriptions of which are circulated for use by CIREM.

traced by it, we see that the two triangles unite, determining the emancipation of man in the universe and his place as an aspect of the divine center; we see that matter receives life only through reflections springing from the opposition that the truth feels from the false, the light from the darkness, and that the life of this matter always depends on two actions; we see that the quaternary of man embraces the six regions of the universe and that, these regions being linked two by two, the power of man exercises a triple quaternary in the abode of his glory."

Louis-Claude de Saint-Martin, who in his commentary refers to both the Bible and the Chinese *kéou-kou,* invites the man of desire to rely on the peripheries that are the "regions" to find the center of the circle of times, his "glorious throne." The challenge is what we call "Awakening," the renunciation of the dream of man's abandonment of his original central position, to find his own deity remaining in the center of everything.

This figure elicited many comments and very diverse interpretations, which is characteristic of a highly operative symbol. Papus, who made the drawing of Louis-Claude de Saint-Martin the seal of the Martinist Order, proposed an interpretation[24] which became an official instruction in the Ritual of the Martinist Order of Teder.[25] Nevertheless, it was François-Charles Barlet,[26] undoubtedly with Stanislas de Guaita (the most brilliant of the Companions of Hierophany), who made the analysis most interesting to us. Indeed, Barlet identifies three worlds, with duality as a characteristic of the lower world, and assigns three senses to

24 *Traité méthodique de science occulte* (Paris: G. Carré, 1891).

25 *Martinist Ritual* by Blitz, attributed to Charles Détré (Teder) (Paris: Dorbon-aine, 1913; Paris: Demeter, 1985; and Aubagne, Fr: Editions de la Tarente, 2009).

26 François-Charles Barlet, pseudonym of Albert Faucheux (1838-1909), was a companion of Papus and Max Théon.

the center, which is relevant: an "original sense," the Absolute, a "definitive sense" which he describes as a "general synthesis," and an "intermediate sense" which is "the common means of resolving all oppositions," a means that makes it possible to traverse duality in order to reach the nondual. Recall that in the ritual, the initiator invokes: "Spirits of the Kingdom, lead me between the two Columns." The non-identification with the play of opposites traces an interval, a way of the heart, that is to say, of the center.

The model proposed by Barlet is not far from that of the ways of awakening. We find in the famous Saint-Martinist figure what we have stated above.

In the center, the point, is our original and ultimate nature, the Absolute, the Great Real, which also determines all forms and all peripheries, manifested or not. The two triangles are the world of essence and the world of energy consciousness. The circle is the world of form. The cross formed by the diameters indicates the horizontal axis of having and doing, which preserves the periphery, and the vertical axis of being which leads to the center. It also indicates the man in whom the equation of consciousness is played out and solved.

The passage from the periphery to the center is the passage from time to non-time, movement to motionlessness, speech-noise to Word-Silence, duality to the nondual.

The figure is drawn on an immaculate white sheet. This whiteness indicates that everything is played out on the "surface" of the Self and that it is necessary to go beyond the nondual experience to reach the Great Real, the Great Nothing, because as long as there is a point, there are potentially, if not manifestly, circles and as long as there is a circle, there is a point and a path to be drawn from the circle to the point.

What Barlet suggests, with three meanings attributed to the center, is that we can apply the figure itself to each of the worlds:

the world of forms, the world of consciousness-energy, and the world of essence; that this model, valid for the Whole, is also relevant for the parts of the Whole.

We could thus give a new interpretation by referring the two intertwined triangles to the world of consciousness-energy and the world of form. From this new analysis, we deduce the paths that lead to Silence. Thus in the man of desire, the world of forms that has its correspondence in the head, the first brain, and the world of energy and consciousness that has its correspondence in the belly, which we now call the second brain, must unite in the heart which is "the common means of resolving all oppositions" of Barlet. It is in the heart, in the center, that the conditions for the emergence of the New Man must be established.

In any case, the universal figure must be passed through and the means of this return to our own divine state are clearly indicated in the ritual: the mask, the cloak, and the cordelier.

Before coming to the evocative power of these three fundamental symbols of Martinism, we must examine a particular point indicated by the ritual.

Signs and accords[27]

The participants in the ceremony are invited to pay attention "to the various manifestations of the incense burning on the embers." We are there at the heart of occultism and at the heart of a dilemma, so much so that the applications of the "theory of correspondences,"[28] such as it is, tend to be transformed into su-

---

27 [Trans.] The word "accord" here refers to the oaths or agreements of initiatory rituals as well as to musical chords. There is no good English equivalent that captures both meanings, so it's been kept in the original French.

28 It is interesting to examine from the Spinozist angle the second kind of knowledge, that of relations (of which mathematics is only one sector), which allows us to leave the first kind of knowledge, that of inadequate ideas, and to come closer to the third kind, that of essences.

perstitions in ill-prepared intelligences, that is to say, among the majority.

To escape the superstitious imprint one must at the same time sense the world as nothing and the world as poetry; to know the true nature of what presents itself, namely the Void; and to understand the infinite variety of possibilities that can all manifest in a being free from conditioning and unidentified with what is presented in the field of experience. When we talk about superstition, we are not talking only about beliefs bordering on foolishness, we are talking about any belief born out of our attachment to the "me" that wants to have the permanent with the impermanent, the true with the false.

Robert Amadou took care to precisely define this theory of correspondences in a particularly courageous essay, *L'occultisme, esquisse d'un monde vivant*,[29] perhaps his most important book, which impacted both the academic world and the esoteric microcosm. "Restoring the occult to culture" is indeed a Herculean challenge in our narrow society. In this book, Robert Amadou defines occultism as "the set of doctrines and practices based on the theory of correspondences" and the theory of correspondences as "the theory according to which every object belongs to a single set and possesses with every other element of this set necessary, intentional, non-temporal, and non-spatial relations."

It is a dualistic approach (there is object and subject) which takes into account the nondual *Real*, indicating the possibility of non-spatial, non-temporal, and intentional relationships, the intention being Being itself. Robert Amadou rightly asks: "Does a universal intention whose analogy of the universe is only expression penetrate all the cosmos?"

The theory of correspondences has the practical and magical

---

29 *L'occultisme, esquisse d'un monde vivant* by Robert Amadou (Saint-Jean-de-la-Ruelle, Fr: Chanteloup, 1987).

consequence that a heightened consciousness can evoke a force by replacing the manifested force with an element that corresponds to it in an analogical mode. Analogy, which is different from similarity, evokes a like nature, which is translated into symbols. It takes into account non-separation. It conceives of the world as a projection of the analogical relations born within human consciousness. Intention, in heightened consciousness, becomes "will," modifies the "dream" of consciousness, and intervenes in the world of harmony that is also the world of signs and accords.

Robert Amadou quotes Eliphas Levi's eloquent poem:

> *Any idea gives birth to an image*
> *And forms are a language.*
> *Every sign expresses a thought*
> *The invisible is in the visible.*

Note that in the center, in the *Real,* the nature of everything is the Void. The theory of correspondences is therefore valid only for the peripheries and, from one periphery to another, for approaching the immutable center. In the absence of the touch of the Absolute, all magic—which goes far beyond the ceremonial, life itself being magic—is wandering in the peripheries of representation. But for those who remember themselves, for those who tend to get closer to their own reality, to the presence of oneself that is presence in the Self, there is a situating of the environment. The environment "comes to order" with heightened consciousness. The universe, "as consciousness and as nothing," responds to the intention of Being and not to the desire of the person. The world becomes a vast poetic and magical dimension to explore, a space of creation in which the operator can experience the play of energy and consciousness. This play is marked by signs and accords, much like on a musical score. The accord is a response of the environment to the alignment body—speech—thought by the silence of being. The sign is an indication of the path that leads to this alignment. From signs to accords, consciousness discovers the path of intervals: the interval between two moments, two phenomena, between two gestures, two speeches, two thoughts, two words, between inhalation and exhalation, between "me" and other, subject and object, between one world and another, to the point of leaving the fictitious continuity of time and phenomena for the real one of the interval, the Nothing, the All.

Signs and accords constitute a language of their own, an energetic language that takes on a different color for each individual and is nuanced from one context to another, while respecting archetypal constants that symbolism has no doubt succeeded in codifying. The language will not be the same in an urban area as in a natural environment. It will be different in the mountains and at sea. However, the signs and accords will echo from one context to another for the same individual, listening *undivided,* the one who is "one." Any "person" who pays attention to possible signs and accords is in a self-hallucinatory process, since the person does not belong to the intention of Being but to the ephemeral and transitory response of the universe. The person, the "me," is part of the decor. Identification with the "person" is an alienation, the primary alienation of which all the others are only extensions. Signs and accords constitute a language only for the one who remembers where he comes from and where he returns, the one for whom the alpha coincides with the omega, the one in whom the intention and the orient tend to merge with Being.

The nomadic alternative

There could be no initiation without a nomadic alternative, without the circulation of elites, shall we say *"élus,"* those who "were chosen by God"—not an almighty and arbitrary God, external to the human being, but on the contrary, Being in the human. That is to make the choice of one's Self rather than of his little "person."

This essential aspect of the initiatory question is often mentioned briefly but is rarely implemented. Yet it is fundamental. Let's see what the ritual says about it, very clearly:

"From now on, unknown and solitary traveler, you will continue to traverse the cycle of the present life. You will submit again to the ruling powers of Space and Time. There you will be the messenger of the Word, the docile agent of the First Cause, the Sower of Truth. In spiritual communion with all your Brothers and Sisters, with the living and with the dead.

"On your way, sowing seeds of light and wisdom, you will continue the initiatory journey. Whenever you see a chance or necessity imposes it, you will knock on a new door. Wherever the star of the Magi shines, you will recognize a new stage. You will seek Knowledge there, and you will seek it everywhere: within the starry firmament, in the evocative symbolism of the constellations, in the yellow parchments, in the reddening of the athanors, as in the arches of the sacred monuments. But you will only encounter Wisdom in the depths of your inner temple, where, according to the promise, in the darkness of the sanctuary, God sometimes speaks to Israel!"

The invitation is strong to go from sanctuary to sanctuary, from library to library, from university to university, from garden to garden, from tradition to tradition, from wisdom to wisdom, from heaven to heaven, so that each of these bright reflections illuminates a corner of our inner temple. This companionship is both external and internal. It is a source of exchange, never of commerce. The multiplication of encounters with traditional forms forces us to grasp the absolute structure that supports them and of which they are a passing expression. The journey confronts the plurality of languages and makes the eloquence of Silence more evident. The nomad is now at home where he is. The traveler thus becomes Prince of God. He is the Anointed, the title of Christ in its Hebrew form, the Anointed being the mark of all the kings of Israel.

The traveler, left to himself, relying only on his own resources and his own solarity,[30] gradually becomes "Prince of himself." He is his own monarch. This sacred solitude is not heavy like the solitude of the excluded. Sacred solitude arises from the disappearance of otherness. Neither "me" nor other: the Real.

The mask, the cloak, the cordelier

Let us again look at the three fundamental symbols of Martinist ceremonial, symbols which at the same time are significant to the consciousness sharpened by the spirit and indicate the initial alliance, which must be updated, between Being and the unidentified individual consciousness.

These three symbols imply a discipline and a *tekhne,*[31] an art and a science of Being.

"With this mask, your worldly personality disappears. You become an unknown, among others equally unknown." This sentence will have particularly marked Martinist initiates. It in-

---

30 [Trans.] Solarity (French, *solarité*): a nature or aspect relating to, or characteristic of, the Sun.

31 François Châtelet: "There is in *tekhne* the idea of technique, of an applied know-how, but also the idea of an art, an invention, of an original production." *Une histoire de la raison* (Paris: du Seuil, 1992). François Châtelet is also the author of an excellent *Histoire de la Philosophie* (Paris: Hachette, 1972).

dicates in fact the key to initiation and clearly designates the obstacle, momentary but tenacious: "the person," the worldly "me,"
in perpetual representation, in demand of recognition and belonging, a demand impossible to satisfy.

Wearing the mask is a powerful behavioral metaphor whose
effect we can measure in the expression of Carnival. The ano-
nymity provided by the mask reminds us that we are nameless.
We were before we were appointed. We will be after our name is
erased. Our name is an accident. What remains is the nameless.

Wearing the mask is an allusion to our present situation. We
are masked, but we made this mask, the conditioned "person,"
our identity by the play of adhesions. This mask is multifacet-
ed. The "person" is composed of multiple little "me's," so many
schemas that more or less fit in an artificial coherence, the personal story or legend. We are not the mask of appearances that
we ostensibly brandish, as is demonstrated cruelly, but with what
lucidity, by Victor Hugo in *The Man Who Laughs.*

We can make the link between the symbolism of the mask and
the prohibition made by the Old Testament[32] about the use and
the worship of the images of God. The Decalogue, which is still
valid in the new covenant, forbids making images.

The current interpretation has led to conflicts as stupid as they
are harmful, even today. It is more interesting to see in this prohibition of the image of God, an invitation not to constitute and
maintain an image of oneself that veils the Real. The true image of God is Christ, then the man who has become Christ in his
true nature. By giving birth to the ego, and by idolizing it, we fall
under the testamentary prohibition. The Old Testament warns
us against the illusion of "me." Adhering to the ego makes us an
idolater.

To wear the mask is first of all to become aware of the situ-

32 See the note on "Image" in the *Dictionnaire encyclopédique du
christianisme ancien,* Volume I (Paris: Cerf, 1990).

ation, which borders on the grotesque, to discover the plural mask of the ego and to disidentify with it, to take advantage of this mask to isolate oneself because, insists the ritual, "it is from yourself, from your very isolation, that you will draw the flame to illuminate your inner life." Once recognized as such, the mask can therefore become an ally. The ego is an enemy only if we confuse it with our reality, but, recognized as a simple function of consciousness and not as an entity, it can become an ally in the service of our interiority.

We have detailed elsewhere[33] a possible protocol for this return to oneself. Recall what the scope of this protocol was in four exercises:

- The division of attention leads to increased consciousness.
- The practice of the Letter A leads to Emptiness.
- The practice of the Sounds leads to the Mastery of the power of creation.
- The practice of the Meditation of Infinity in the Body leads to Fusion.
- The whole, by the presence Here and Now, allows Autonomy. Autonomous means *autosnomos,* "who gives himself his own law." It means leaving the circle of identifications, dilutions, representations, and mental crystallizations, to reach the Center where simply "I am" or "I remain," no longer "to be lived," but to live.

The practice of the letter A, simple and excessively difficult, is considered the most internal practice of many traditions, in the East as in the West, although it is taught in its first form to all. From this practice arises, in fact, both the highest metaphysics and internal alchemy. All the traditional teachings are collected in the letter A. This sole sound, A, explains all of the Real and constitutes the true transmission.

---

33 *Éveil et incohérisme* by Rémi Boyer (La Bégude de Mazenc, Fr: Arma Artis, 2005.)

The important thing here is that its practice leads to Silence, the place and vector of Realization, and that its effects are quickly tangible and almost measurable:

- The verification of a real practice is always behavioral:
  - control of the environment;
  - the art of "bending" time;
  - development of energy and solarity;
  - greater serenity.

The Martinist ritual makes explicit reference to the letter A when the initiator, to invoke, "raises his right hand, the thumb squared," a sign traditionally associated with the sound A from which all other sounds flow. This detail is of utmost importance. It shows us the required state of presence in oneself, the need for silence which alone can render the word creative. Invocation uttered in the midst of noise is just another noise. Louis-Claude de Saint-Martin suggests in *Of Errors and Truth* that the world is only in disharmony because of our ignorance of the real name of each object. We recover the myth of the Lost Word which is only emanated Silence. The right word is the word before the word, the unpronounceable word. The invocation that springs from Silence, inscribed in the conscious breath, carries within it a pure idea, a creative thought. In this case, and in this case only, in this alignment with Being, energy follows thought. The Word creates. The initiator can then create, receive and constitute, as the formula of consecration affirms: "I create you, receive you, and constitute you an Unknown Superior."

Whatever the protocol implemented, which refers us to the prerequisites of initiation, it always aims to reduce and then stop the internal dialogue, the chaotic flow of thoughts, to access the interval. Behind the mask, recapitulation is possible, not only the psychological recapitulation that aims to learn from the past, but the energetic recapitulation that makes it possible to reappropriate all the energy deployed to maintain the past, project a future, and develop a personal history. Folding time, behind the mask, thus introduces an art of "de-facement," to the awareness of our headlessness. Where we thought we had a face, there is only the infinite Void and its fullness, as has been magnificently demonstrated, by renewing the almost universal tradition of headlessness, by Douglas Harding.[34]

The initiate is an unmasked being. Unmasked, he is faceless and therefore can not appear. If the Martinist initiate wears a mask, it is the better to tear off all the masks that duality has led him to confuse with his real identity.

Another dimension of the mask is the hermetic language. The mask invites us to appropriate the sciences of Hermes. François Rabelais reminds us in a scene that brings together Panurge, prototype of the quester on an initiatory journey, and Thaumaste, who evokes Mercury and to whom Panurge replies, "You spoke a mask." "To speak a mask" is to make use of the hermetic language, of the twilight poetry of the adepts.

Before putting on the mask, before allowing himself to be unmasked by his own divine nature, the initiate must learn to protect himself. "Learn then to enfold yourself in the mysterious cloak" suggests the ritual. But what cloak is it?

Thanks to the similar names, we immediately think of the famous cloak of St. Martin. This man, born of pagan parents in 316 in present-day Hungary, converted to Christianity after sharing his cloak with a poor man dying of cold. Later, in 361, he founded the first monastery in the West, the monastery of Ligugé, near Poitiers. St. Martin has become the very symbol of giving and sharing, a symbol on which it is useless to insist except to say, with Robert Amadou, that Beneficence and Benevolence constitute an equivalent of theurgy.[35]

---

34 See in particular *To Be and Not to Be* (London: Shollond Trust, 2015).

35 This within the setting of the Rectified Scottish Rite and its Beneficent Knights of the Holy City.

Without neglecting St. Martin, it is above all the cloak of Elijah that may interest us here. The cloak of Elijah manifests, even
more than it symbolizes, the double anointing of the Spirit. Elijah,
the great prophet of Israel in the eleventh century BCE, veiled his
face with this cloak when, on Mount Horeb, the Lord approached
him, thereby indicating another function of the cloak which not
only isolates us and hides us from hostile eyes, but also preserves
us from too great a Light, too great a Presence. Certain Awak-
enings consume an ill-prepared physical apparatus and psychic
system. With Elijah, the cloak is also a vector of transmission. We
are approaching the true transmission from Silence to Silence,
from Being to Being, from Spirit to Spirit. Elisha, his disciple, a
simple farmer, received the anointing of Elijah when he "cast his
cloak upon him" (1 Kings 19:19) and says to Elisha, in effect: "If
you can follow me, you will not only become my successor, but I
will give you my anointing." This sentence strongly suggests the
distinction between the temporal lineage, manifested in succession, and the vertical line, accessible by anointing. It is the power
of the Free Spirit who, playing with the separation, with the two,
lives through the initiator and the initiate. It is this "crossing" of
duality that constitutes a transmission. This transmission makes
him a "monk." Elijah, whom the *Pistis Sophia* affirms to have returned as John the Baptist, is, according to Sister Éliane Poirot,
the archetype of the monk.[36] The etymology of the word, Greek
or Latin, refers us to loneliness, to *monos,* "alone," not only amidst
the world, or despite the world, but alone with it, because not
separate. The Unknown Superior, through asceticism and discipline, through his unconditional commitment without which no

---

36 *Elie, archétype du moine,* Sister Éliane Poirot, O.C.D., Saint Elijah
Monastery, Spiritualité orientale n° 65 (Abbaye de Bellefontaine: 1995).
Les prophètes Elie et Elisée dans la littérature chrétienne ancienne, Sister
Éliane Poirot (Turnhout, Be: Brepols and Abbaye de Bellefontaine, 1997).

realization is possible, is indeed a "monk" in the world, with the world, and through the world. Finally, the prophet Elijah does not fail to evoke the figure of Elias Artista, the Archangel of the Rose-Croix. The cloak of Elijah becomes the thrill of Elias Artista of whom Sedir[37] gave us the intuition:

> Elias Artista is the angel of the Rose-Croix. No one can know who he is, even the one he rests on. All that can be said is that it is an attractive, harmonizing force and that it tends to unite individuals into one homogeneous body.[38, 39]

Once again, reintegration is thought of as an abandonment of all separation, by the reunification of all individuals, not "persons," into one entity. Sedir goes on to quote Stanislas de Guaita:

> He is not the Light; but, like St. John the Baptist, his mission is to bear witness to the Light of glory, which must shine forth from a new heaven on a rejuvenated earth. Let him show himself by counsels of strength and clear the pyramid of holy traditions, disfigured by those heterogeneous layers of detritus and plaster that twenty centuries have heaped upon it! And finally, through him, the ways are opened to the advent of the glorious Christ, in the great halo of whom will vanish—his work being accomplished— the precursor of the times to come, the human expression of the holy Paraclete, the daimon of science and freedom, of integral wisdom and justice: Elias Artista!

---

37 Paul Sedir, whose real name was Yvon Le Loup (1871-1926), was an influential esotericist in the entourage of Papus and a surprisingly prolific author. He was one of the leaders of the Martinist Order and the Kabbalistic Order of the Rose-Croix.

38 Elias Artista is therefore also the destroyer of the illusion that separates and divides.

39 *Histoire et Doctrines des Rose-Croix* by Paul Sedir (Paris: Bibliothèque des Amitiés Spirituelles, 1932).

The function of the witness, not only of the Light, but here "in the Light," the crossing of the sclerotic forms, the call to the Paraclete, to an entirety that is only conceivable in Self and by Self, the distinction between traditions and ways, are all characteristic of the philosophies of awakening.

Finally, Sedir continues:

> Elias Artista is an adaptation of the Biblical Elijah, who must return at the end of time with Enoch, so that they may fulfill their role as witnesses in the universal binary. It would be premature to say who Elias Artista was, or who he will be. All that is useful to know is that this name denotes a form of the Spirit of intelligence.

Armand Toussaint[40] attributed to the cloak the same symbolic value as the knight's armor, which was for him of an energetic nature. He often referred to the armor and helmet of Athena, the material of which he affirmed is that energy generated by the full activity of the energy centers, or chakras, in the body. We find in classical Christian iconography, Catholic or Orthodox, many indications of how to build this armor or cloak. The concept developed by Armand Toussaint is reminiscent of certain martial traditions that develop a cloak of energy capable of absorbing blows and even returning the destructive effects on the opponent.

But it was to the kabbalah taught by his master, Serge Marcotoune of Kiev, that Armand Toussaint referred in order to constitute the twenty-two pieces of armor.

In a table, Armand Toussaint wanted both to synthesize the mantric practice (based here on Hebrew, but which finds its

---

40 Armand Toussaint (1895-1994), a prominent figure in the Martinist scene, was the founder and head of the Martinist Order of the Knights of Christ from 1971, when it was founded, until his death in 1994. See the Appendix for a portrait of Armand Toussaint.

equivalent in Latin or ancient Greek) that allows the development of the armor, or the cloak, and to summarize the alchemical process that leads to the Great Work. These are simple indications for a grand design.[41]

Alpha: "Know thyself..."
The initiate seeks his Unknown within himself.

Aleph............1.....................The will of unity (Alchemical Salt)

Beth..............2.....................The science of the inner binary

Gimel..........3.....................The positive inner synthesis

Daleth..........4.....................The quaternary of realization: *Sta—Solve—Coagula—Multiplica*

He................5.....................The inspired will, the era of the Popes

Vav..............6.....................The choice of the Path between spiritual Clarity and Darkness

Zain.............7.....................The triumph or failure of spirit over matter

Cheth..........8.....................The search and acquisition of inner balance

Teth.............9.....................The integration of enriching experiences through mystical techniques: *Look to see—Listen to hear—Make the inner Silence:* "*Vide, Audi, Tace*"

---

41 In the appendix, the reader will find under the title *Spiritual Exercises for Bears and Knights* a set of exercises based on this work by Armand Toussaint.

Delta: "...you will know the others..."

The initiate in manifestation in the world, his habits and customs, learns to live there by experiencing the attacks that strengthen him. He dwells in the world, but he does not identify with the world, nor with worlds.

Yod.............. 10 ....The time, the opportunity to experiment in the vortices of the world.

Kaph............. 11 or 20..........The occult force.

Lamed.......... 12 or 30..........The sacrifice that the initiate makes by accepting constraints to make them serve his spiritual progression.

Mem............. 13 or 40..........The conquest of death or the division of consciousness, the change of dimension (Alchemical Sulfur).

Nun .... 14 or 50 ....Energetic recapitulation, new associations, the creation of a favorable future karma.

Samekh........ 15 or 60 ....The attack of Baphomet, emotional reactions.

A'in .... 16 or 70 ....The shelter or the ruin.

Pe .... 17 or 80 ....The star of hope.

Tzadi .... 18 or 90 ....The disappointment caused by treacherous attacks.

Omega: "...and the Gods."

The initiate projects his love of the Beautiful, the True, and the Good into the world.

Qoph............. 19 or 100 ......The inner light has come into being by the inner silence.

Resh.............. 20 or 200 .....Time, Rebirth, Renewal, Longevity, Immortality.

Shin .... 21 or 300 ...... Victory in the very Kingdom of
the Prince of this world. The Ini-
tiate, Fool of Spiritual Light, pursues his Way in his mystic intoxication, indifferent to the attacks
of evil: he is the *Mat* in the Tarot
of the visionaries of the Middle
Ages, dead to the world.

Tav .... 22 or 400 ..... The Great Alchemical and Spir-
itual Work or the reward of the
Man-God, replica of the God-
Man, the New Man, Christ, the
Panacea, the Philosopher's Stone.

Kaph final .... 23 or 500 ...... The active Will supported by experience and hope.

Mem final .... 24 or 600 ..... The second Death with penetration into the World of the Spirit
by the judicious, liberated, and
sacrificial choice. The double Essence.

Nun final ..... 25 or 700 ...... The triumphal Will, in the storm,
to wash away the karma of the
world *(peccata mundi)*. The triple
Essence.

Pe final .... 26 or 800 ..... The hope of redemption that
induces spiritual balance in the
world. The quadruple Essence.

Tzadi final ... 27 or 900 ..... The discovery of a great Syn-
thesis. Higher Initiation of the
Rose-Croix (or Bodhisattva). The
Quintessence.

New Aleph…28 or 1000 …Liberation. The birth of the creative sun. Unification in the
Breast of God. The Reintegration of the Ascended Master. The
Millennium.

Let us remember that the states mentioned above, places-states
as Claude Bruley[42] would say, are not states of the "person," of the
body-mind system, but of the differentiated states of increased
consciousness in Silence. It is under the cloak of Silence that "the
initiate seeks his Unknown within himself." In this path towards
the One, we will note the initial importance of the will to unity,
a will that we find active and then triumphant throughout the
initiatory process.

Louis-Claude de Saint-Martin was neither a Kabbalist, nor an
alchemist, nor an astrologer. He was even suspicious of alchemy
until his encounter with the works of Jacob Bœhme. However,
the three components of the *Trivium hermeticum* (astrology,[43]
magic, and alchemy), fully became Martinist sciences from the
founding of the Martinist Order by Papus. Likewise, Kabbalah
imposed itself as a favored subject for study among Martinists.
There is no incompatibility between Saint-Martin's thought and
these operative domains. The doctrine that founded the system
of the Primitive Cult, as it was established in the framework of the
Order of Knight Masons Elus Coëns of the Universe by Martines
de Pasqually, is specific to a movement parallel to the kabbalistic
current and equally ancient.[44] The high Bœhmian mysticism that

---

42 *Le Grand Œuvre comme fondement d'une spiritualité laïque. Le chemin de l'individuation,* by Claude Bruley (Cordes-sur-Ciel, Fr: Rafael de
Surtis, 2008).

43 Or more generally any form of divination that discerns, illuminates, and interprets analogical correspondences.

44 Read the introduction of *Les leçons de Lyon aux élus coëns* by Robert Amadou, *L'Esprit des Choses* collection (Paris: Dervy, 1999).

we find in Saint-Martin fits perfectly with the sciences of Hermes. Illuminism finally comes to underline the purpose of the higher sciences by recalling what the ultimate plan of God is for the human being. Louis-Claude de Saint-Martin underwent the operations to identify what is essential, independent of forms: Silence, the very deep intimacy of the human being with God, the Real, the Absolute, the possibility of actualizing this intimacy here and now to become Christ, which, symbolically, passes through the experience of the mask, the cloak, and the cordelier, an experience that should be mastered before relinquishing it.

After the mask and the cloak, the initiate receives "the cordelier, symbol of the magic circle and the chain of the tradition." We have already discussed earlier, with regard to the Past Masters, the question of lineages, horizontal and vertical, temporal and timeless, a question to which the symbolism of the cordelier refers. We will not return to it except to specify a few points of importance.

The cordelier, more than the symbol of a link with an external third party, surrounds our kidneys and stomach, the ocean of energy. It goes from ourselves to ourselves. It indicates that everything is in us, that we give birth to the world, and that it is up to us to stop feeding a world that is lost in the endless elasticity of time, thus recalling the dispersed energy and letting it stand like a pillar to support Heaven. Stop generating the forms in order to nourish Christ within us, our own divinity, "the seed of the future god" according to the ritual.

The cordelier has a very special protective function if we are to believe the myth of Gawain and the Green Knight, a little-used episode among the legends of the Grail. Accepting to lose his head, for having indulged in desire, the Knight is saved by the belt given to him by the Lady he desired, who is here Sophia. The cordelier does not preserve the "person" who alone is destined for the sacrifice, it preserves intimacy with Being.

Once our divine headlessness has been found behind the mask, once our armor is constituted or reconstituted, once we are consciously pregnant with ourselves, with our own original and ultimate reality, we can then become truly an Unknown Superior.

"Please remove from the new member of our Order the three symbols we have just bestowed," the initiator asks. We must always, sooner or later, lay down arms and protections, because the use of these maintains division and duality. We have to give up the "skillful means," a Buddhist would say. We must put aside what frees us in order to be free even from liberation. The Martinist initiate leaves the three symbols, the three operative tools, which are the mask, the cloak, and the cordelier, in this true nudity, to receive the white collar of the Unknown Superiors of the Order and its secular Pantacle of which he now possesses the knowledge.

Every ritual is an operative metaphor. It is easy to observe the depth of it and the definitive scope it comprises. This is not a matter of the Martinist Order, a human and ephemeral structure like all the orders that claim to be initiatory, but of the invisible Assembly of the Friends of God, the inhabitants of the High Country, the Masters of the Kingdom of the Center, Immortals banished and finally returned. The term "Unknown Superior" designates a grade only by default. Just like the beautiful appellations of Rose-Croix or Réau-Croix, it evokes a "superior" consciousness, freed from all conditions, and therefore from every name. It is "unknown" and "unknowable." It *is*.

The Unknown Superior has crossed the world of duality to access the nondual.

The Johannite reference

The Martinist ritual specifies that the Gospel of Saint John will be open to Chapter 1 on the altar:

1. In the beginning was the Word, and the Word was with God, and the Word was God.
2. The same was in the beginning with God.
3. All things were made by him; and without him was not any thing made that was made.
4. In him was life; and the life was the light of men.
5. And the light shineth in darkness; and the darkness comprehended it not.
6. There was a man sent from God, whose name was John.
7. The same came for a witness, to bear witness of the Light, that all men through him might believe.
8. He was not that Light, but was sent to bear witness of that Light.
9. That was the true Light, which lighteth every man that cometh into the world.
10. He was in the world, and the world was made by him, and the world knew him not.
11. He came unto his own, and his own received him not.
12. But as many as received him, to them gave he power to become the sons of God, even to them that believe on his name:
13. Which were born, not of blood, nor of the will of the flesh, nor of the will of man, but of God.
14. And the Word was made flesh, and dwelt among us, (and we beheld his glory, the glory as of the only begotten of the Father,) full of grace and truth.
15. John bare witness of him, and cried, saying, This was he of whom I spake, He that cometh after me is preferred before me: for he was before me.

16. And of his fulness have all we received, and grace for grace.
17. For the law was given by Moses, but grace and truth came by Jesus Christ.
18. No man hath seen God at any time, the only begotten Son, which is in the bosom of the Father, he hath declared him.

We are not going to make here an exegesis of this highly poetic text which holds a special place in the Gospels. Let's just emphasize how it illustrates our point:

The prologue of the Gospel of Saint John speaks of creation, therefore of the temporal world, "turned towards God," mirror of Being. Darkness forms the "person" conditioned by the play of identifications. John is the witness, the one who comes to bear witness to the sacred within the "person." He bears witness to the Light, to the Word, to the Christ, emanating from Silence and present even within form, even within conditioning. Christ, obviously prior to the witness, is nondual permanence even in duality, a permanence of which we have an intuition because it is attached to our own reality. If the "person" cannot see God, the One in us, the *undivided,* hidden in multiplicity but announced and enlightened by the witness, reveals Him to us and leads us there.

The ascending path of return, of reintegration, is inscribed in the downward movement from the center to the peripheries, from the One to the number. By retreating from the outermost phenomenal peripheries towards the immutable center, by going from the complex to the simple, by ascending from the number to the One, the Initiate, Hidden King, appears in all his fullness and glory.

This is suggested by the beautiful central invocation of this ceremonial, the invocation which founds the rite:

"May this one Light, emanating from these several luminaries, reveal to us the mysterious Power of the One who sustains our particular temple, which we are about to raise to the glory of God and of his Son, the Word, Eternal and Uncreated, our Lord. For in the beginning was the Word, and the Word was with God, and the Word was God. All things were made by Him, and without Him was not any thing made that was made. In Him was life, and the life was the Light of men. And the Light shineth in Darkness, and the Darkness comprehendeth it not."

The triangle of darkness, power—territory—reproduction, becomes vertical under the action of the triangle of Light, Silence—Word—Freedom or Universal Father-Mother (Silence)—Son (Word)—Holy Spirit (Freedom). The will to Be initiates this reversal, but it cannot be accomplished without Grace, as the prologue suggests. The initiate is first of all in imitation, of Christ very often (and always for Martinists), then in invention. He invents himself, self-generates as a new Christ. The serpentine forces scattered throughout manifestation gather in the center to orient themselves according to "the Higher Sense."

6   The Free Initiator

"My sect is Providence, my proselytes are myself, my worship is justice; for a long time this has been the font of all my ideas, all my sentiments, and all my doctrine; the more I advance in age, the more these principles and movements are fortified in me, because the food my spirit takes is absolutely of the same kind; it is not surprising that this relation and this correspondence leave me with effects analogous to them."

Louis-Claude de Saint-Martin

THE MARTINIST ORDER IS, NOT THE LEAST among its other peculiarities, one of the very few initiatory orders to implement "free initiators" (to varying extents, depending upon the times and branches of the Order).

The formula is ambivalent. Indeed, by realization, rather than by definition, an initiate is free; *a fortiori,* it is to be hoped, an initiator. As we saw in the previous chapter, the initiate is only freedom. The tragedy would be that an initiator, an initiate, is not freed. It would be a denial of his own nature and his own fulfillment.

To qualify the initiate as "free" is therefore an abuse of language which aims, behind the redundancy, to insist on the qualification required to initiate.

Most Martinist orders have finally renounced free initiators, due to concern for centralization, for politics, for Masonic contagion, and sometimes for lucidity. This renunciation is very damaging.

The Martinist ritual, however, conveys the principle of the free initiator, even when it does not use the title. Thus, in the *Rituel de l'Ordre martiniste prepared by Teder*,[45] a careful examination of the words addressed by the consecrator to the one who is called to receive the "Honorary Degree of Unknown Superior, Great Architect" reveals the basis of the free initiator:

Brother Unknown Superior, you are now ready to leave our School. From this day on, all relationships with your Initiator must cease, except for the relationship of a Brother with another Brother of his rank. Any other relationship with your Unknown Superiors of today, your equals of tomorrow, must cease and not be renewed, because every member of our Order must remain a personal entity. For this reason, the Initiator has the duty to suspend all initiatory relations with each of his Initiates, as soon as this Initiate becomes himself an Initiator. The growth of the Order is thus analogous to cell diffusion by segmentation: one cell contains another only for a very short time. The mother cell divides, giving rise to cells which in turn quickly become mother cells. The Order of Unknown Superiors is organized in such a way as to leave the greatest independence to each of its constituent elements, while maintaining the strongest cohesion of the whole. Human freedom must never be restricted, and the Order always works with the free and absolute consent of the Members who unite for a particular work.

Each Unknown Superior may, if he so desires, be an active member of a Lodge or remain independent. He must be an Unknown, theoretically if not really, among his colleagues, except for

---

45 *Rituel martiniste* by Blitz, attributed to Charles Détré (Teder) (Paris: Dorbon-Aíné, 1913; Paris: Déméter, 1985; and Aubagne: Éditions de la Tarente, 2009).

his Initiator who constitutes the only link by which he is united to the Order. Consequently, it is incumbent upon any Unknown Superior to be able to communicate rapidly with those whom he has initiated, whatever their degree. He thus forms the point of intersection between other groups and his own, and really represents the most important organ of the Order. Ultimately a member can never really be an Unknown Superior before he is an initiator and has transmitted the Light.

The advantages of such an organization are considerable and it is unnecessary to list them all. The most important and main thing is the absolute freedom left to each member to develop the teachings of the Order on his own, according to his own aptitudes and social preferences, etc. In fact, each Initiator is free to adapt to any particular branch of human knowledge and to introduce, in his work in the Lodge, exoteric differences, while keeping the principles of the esotericism of Martinism. Another advantage of this system is the difficulty, in intolerant countries, of destroying the society—given the absolute impossibility of holding all the threads of it. A traitor, a spy, or anyone else who violates his oath can only divulge the name of a member, his Initiator, and he can never prevent the Order from developing other groups of whose existence he does not know.

Here, my brother, is a summary of your new duties. Will you give your word of honor, before this respectable Lodge, to fulfill your duties as an Unknown Superior, with the greatest fidelity and the greatest promptness?

What immediately strikes the reader is that the new initiator is clearly put out of the School, in accordance with the double principle of the nomadic alternative and the circulation of elites. The goal of any school, whether profane or initiatory, is indeed that its students become one day, the sooner the better, able to do without its services and that they be able to create their own school.

We can only note that the first concern of the orders that claim to be initiatory in our time is not this. They favor quantity rather than quality and want to keep as many members as possible for mercantile, financial, or political reasons. Their leaders have great difficulty using the skills of the members who have developed the way within themselves and who they believe are overshadowing them. It invariably ends in conflict, rupture, or exclusion.

Those who thought of organizing Martinism were surprisingly aware of what was at stake. The Companions of Hierophany were all strong personalities and brilliant individuals. Each mastered at least one traditional discipline. Everyone needed a space large enough to work. Initiation aims at the development of the individual's solarity, his radiance. It takes a particular organization for many solar entities to radiate without interfering or colliding, and this organization cannot be modeled on secular hierarchies, but can rather approach what Alvin Toffler called "adhocracies,"[46] collegial systems capable of transforming themselves according to the situations and actions in progress. This collegial and congenial model exists in the initiatory milieu within a few internal colleges, thus bringing together a limited number of individuals who will be considered to have gone beyond archaic identifications. This is the model adopted within the Order of Unknown Superiors. The strength of the Companions of Hierophany is to have found a model of non-centralized organization that can develop without limit and is able to preserve the principle of initiatory solarity, applicable to external or semi-internal initiatory orders.[47]

---

46 *Future Shock* by Alvin Toffler (New York: Random House, 1970).

47 See the typology of initiatory societies presented in *Freemasonry as a Way of Awakening* by Rémi Boyer (Bayonne NJ: Rose Circle, 2020).

This organization, based on a breath of energy, light, and intelligence (within the entities that are groups, lodges, and orders) also presents a societal advantage. Its network development, this weaving or this meshing of the esoteric terrain, makes the order difficult to apprehend or to eradicate in the event of confrontation with a totalitarian government which, always, red or brown, ends up attacking initiatory societies by prohibiting and pursuing every "secret society." Initiation is essentially liberatory[48] and initiatory societies are still considered subversive even by so-called democracies. The composer Olivier Greif explained to me at length one day that the only true revolution was spiritual and interior, but that its consequences extended to all fields of human experience. By "spirituality" he meant the way of awakening and not the protocols of falling asleep that are most religions and movements qualified as spiritual. Initiation disrupts society and its political, religious, social, economic, academic, and scientific institutions by forcing it to look at the lies on which it is constructed. That is why initiatory societies always have an interest in preserving themselves and choosing discretion. If an apparent tolerance towards them reigns in the democracies of the planet, this tolerance is fragile and a new witch hunt is always possible, as demonstrated in France by the liberticidal activity of anti-cult groups incapable of discernment, great masters of amalgamation and confusion, promoters of laws that violate fundamental freedoms, as denounced by international human rights bodies. The legal system of common law is largely sufficient to tackle sectar-

---

48 Let us quote Robert Amadou about the Freemasonry of Memphis-Misraim: "Memphis-Misraim lives from the liberatory spirit; she thus joins the other illuminist rites of Freemasonry, that is evident, and she agrees in thought, I believe, with Masonry one and many, indivisible in spite of appearances, which for me is liberatory." Extract from an interview with Ludovic Marcos, published in the review *Arcana* of the Grand Orient of France, No. 4, first half of 2002.

ian excesses. It was not necessary to develop concepts as dangerous as mental manipulation.

Another point on which this ritual insists is worthy of note. It is "the absolute freedom left to each member to develop by himself the teachings of the Order, according to his own aptitudes and social preferences, etc." The initiator is supposed to have discovered the absolute structure behind traditional forms and disciplines. He has progressed along the path of initiation, and has realized it, from the moment he grasped that whatever the tradition, whatever the discipline, whatever the exercise or the practice, it is always the same free posture of the mind that is at work, the same stake, the verticalization of consciousness in the field of energy in motion. One who is persuaded to work in different forms cannot progress, lost in the meanderings of comparison and commentary. This absolute, formless structure can take them all, old or contemporary, traditional or avant-garde. The initiator can thus put on this structure habits adapted to the situation, in order to break habit within the identified consciousness of his initiables, and to create the interval in the representation that allows the divine surprise of Awakening. The initiator is an artist.

> In fact, each Initiator is free to adapt to any particular branch of human knowledge and to introduce into his work in the Lodge exoteric differences, while keeping the principles of the esotericism of Martinism.

The initiator can borrow from all fields of culture. Experience shows that, without this transversality, initiates tend to crystallize the teaching received in truth or in dogma, including the teaching of non-identification or erudition which often turns out to be a handicap. The difficulty, for the initiator, consists in never allowing the initiate to rely on a formal, thus external, certainty, in order to allow an internal, informal, and indisputable reference to advance within him that emanates from Being itself. The initiate must remain "at the forefront of himself."[49]

This leads us to warn once again against the confusion between the initiatory paths, which relate to the Real, and initiatory orders, which relate to the human. This current confusion perhaps explains why Louis-Claude de Saint-Martin was wary of initiatory orders, although he spent his life in them; why Master Philippe said he was resolutely hostile to their activities while he himself was then inspiring several leaders of initiatory orders; why Robert Amadou repeated to whoever wanted to hear him that, at best, initiatory orders render service. The initiatory ways emerge naturally in the silence of the unidentified consciousness, they deploy energetically along serpentine paths that lead the initiate to where he is to go. The "things" are set up around him, firmly anchored in his own solarity, in his own radiant Presence. Initiatory orders are temporary forms conditioned by culture, intended to be momentary vehicles of these ways or, more precisely, to offer a containing and creative framework to those who seek a real way just as to those who, having found it, let it unfold in their consciousness. They must accompany the initiates to create the conditions of the quest that allow the way to emerge in the unidentified consciousness of the quester. They create the conditions of initiation, but do not give initiation, contrary to a firmly established but erroneous belief. Initiation belongs exclusively to the Self.

Would not the prototype of the Free Initiator for the Christian West be Jesus of Nazareth? Not the one modeled by the Roman

49 See the "Premier manifest incohériste" in Rémi Boyer's *Éveil et incohérisme* (La Bégude de Mazenc, Fr: Arma Artis, 2005) or *Le discours de Lisbonne* by the same author (Cordes sur Ciel, Fr: Rafael de Surtis, 2003).

Church, not the one repackaged by the Gnostics, but the one that, according to Claude Bruley, "got rid of the conjunction with the God of Israel,"[50] has freed himself from all temporal belonging, all ancestral lineage as a spiritual lineage, to establish or restore his own primordial nature, to become again a "complete being endowed with a proper name and a will that is no longer subject to, or dependent on, the collective consciousness."

"Ultimately a member can never really be an Unknown Superior before he is an initiator and has transmitted the Light," says the ritual. This sentence is an additional reminder to nonduality. To not transmit the Light would maintain a duality, a separation between shadow and Light. To transmit, that is to say, to let the Light spread, is to recognize that there is neither "me" nor any other, neither initiate nor profane, and that everything is Light. This sentence, in a more pragmatic way, also suggests that without sharing, without flow, there can be no ascension. To preserve, to retain, is to freeze and be frozen. To keep is to fill oneself, while the first quality of the initiate is the Void which is his true nature. To transmit the Light is to stay on the axis, in the field and the song of Being, rather than descending the rungs of the horizontal scale of having and doing.

It emerges from this ritual that the plurality of Martinist orders or branches of the Martinist Order is a logical consequence of the fundamental principles established for the initiators. It is a guarantee of the independence of this major current of illuminism, of its creativity, and of its freedom. Of course, there are sometimes abuses. Certainly there have been, and occasionally there will be, unworthy constitutions, rather less than in other currents that are very centralized. But the benefits are considerable and cannot

---

50 *Le Grand Œuvre comme fondement d'une spiritualité laïque. Le chemin vers l'Individuation* by Claude Bruley, p. 387 (Cordes sur Ciel, Fr: Rafael de Surtis, 2008).

be called into question by these few disadvantages. One can only regret that the principle of Free Initiators is not more preserved.

On the occasion of the bicentenary of the death of Louis-Claude de Saint-Martin, the International Center for Martinist Research and Studies (CIREM) has released a *Charter for XXIst Century Martinist Orders,* intended to recall what Martinism is and the principles discussed in this chapter and the previous one.

This charter was drawn up from the proposals of Robert Amadou, taken almost *in extenso* by a college brought together by CIREM. Robert Amadou, initially in favor of this project, later considered that it was perhaps not appropriate to disseminate this charter, the times being turbulent. Often in perfect agreement with Robert Amadou, who did not elaborate his position, I considered this time that we did not have to take into account short-term data, the charter insisting on the substance rather than on the forms and seeking a long-term effect. CIREM disseminated the charter that was initially received unevenly in Martinist circles. Some ancient branches seized it, others ignored it. Some recent branches relied on its statements, others rejected it. A number of lodges put it under study, including some within branches of orders rather hostile to its diffusion. CIREM received, and still receives, numerous testimonies from members and from managers of lodges to speak of the contribution of the charter to their reflection and the quality of their work.

The charter obviously disturbs the branches, which are ultimately few in number, that have locked themselves into an operation denying initiatory freedom. It was also designed for this. Martinism, by its recruitment, tends to "masonize." Whenever it allows itself to become institutionalized, it runs the risk of seeing the letter prevail over the spirit as is already the case in Freemasonry. The charter allows aspirants and initiates to be aware of what Martinist initiation requires and to be demanding about the quality of the work offered, as well as on the guarantees that the Martinist framework must provide.

Essentially, while respecting each of the forms that the Martinist work can take, it strongly suggests a return to Louis-Claude de Saint-Martin, who remains insufficiently studied and practiced in most Martinist branches around the world.

Here is the complete text of this charter, as it was distributed on the occasion of the bicentenary of the disappearance of the Unknown Philosopher.

7 Charter for XXIst Century Martinist Orders[51]

Introduction

Throughout the past century, the history of the Order and Martinist Orders remained rich and eventful. If the Order founded by Papus branched out into many branches, this tree was the fruit of the very principle of the Martinist initiation, free initiation, in line, from individual to individual.

Martinist circles, groups, lodges, and orders were, throughout the past century, crucibles that allowed illuminist, occultist, and hermetic currents to endure or to flourish. The freedom, the tolerance, the spirit of research which dominated the Martinist movement, despite some inevitable vicissitudes, allowed many questers to find themselves, independently of their particular paths, in a true companionship under the aegis of the Unknown Philosopher.

The Martinist Order also knew how to welcome into its midst other currents to preserve them and help them experience a new development.

Today, so that this state of mind remains, and that what is alive

51 "Martinist Order" means any order called "Martinist," whatever its subsidiary qualification.

does not become frozen, there are inscribed in this *Charter for XXIst Century Martinist Orders* the simple principles that have contributed to the influence of Martinism since Papus.

The adoption of this Charter is free, it confers no rights—only the duties that stem from ethics. No one will have to give an account of it, except to himself and to Providence.

1—*According to Saint Martin*

I

"My sect is Providence, my proselytes are me; my cult is justice."

"...I am astonished that you found me so infatuated with my feeble merit that I could give my name to my old school or any other. Institutions sometimes serve to mitigate the ills of man, more often to increase them, never to cure them."

"The only initiation I seek with all the ardor of my soul is that by which we can enter into the heart of God and bring the heart of God into us, to make an indissoluble marriage there, which makes us friends, the brother and the husband of our divine repairer. There is no other mystery in arriving at this holy initiation than to sink deeper and deeper into the depths of our being and to not let go until we have managed to feel the living and life-giving root, because then all the fruits which we were to bear according to our kind naturally occur in us and outside us, as we see happen to our earthly trees, because they are adherent to their particular root and they do not cease to raise up sap."

2

Louis-Claude de Saint-Martin devoted a large part of his life to the initiatory orders that he frequented, but he did not found any and kept a due reservation for all. Through his work, he initiated a major current of Christian Illuminist thought and invited people to come together in fraternity of spirit. On the verge of death, Louis-Claude de Saint-Martin "exhorted all those around him to put their trust in Providence, and to live among themselves as brothers, in the sentiments of the Gospel."

II—*According to Papus*

1

Papus founded the Martinist Order in several stages:
- 1884-1885: the first initiations.
- 1887: the first lodge.
- 1887-1890: establishment of the Martinist Order, drafting of statutes and instruction books.
- 1891: constitution of the first Supreme Council.

2

The initiation of 1882 to which Papus refers, and that which Augustine Chaboseau places for him in 1886, initiations which they transmitted to each other in 1888, remain uncertain in their nature and as to their circumstances. They took a different and barely ritualistic form. It is the initiation of Papus, not Papus-Chaboseau, that since the foundation of the Martinist Order constitutes the "Martinist" initiation.

III—According to the Order

1

Papus conceived and defined the Martinist Order as both an initiatory order and a school of moral chivalry[52] and Christian occultism.

The Christianity of the Martinist Order is marked by Martines de Pasqually's doctrine of universal Reintegration as well as by Saint-Martin's cardiac way of internal transmutation, and the occultism is "the set of doctrines and practices based on the theory according to which every object belongs to a unique set and possesses with every other element of this set necessary, intentional, non-temporal, and non-spatial relations,"[53] the so-called correspondence theory.

2

Papus and the Companions of Hierophany were animated by the spirit of research, non-dogmatic speculation finding its foundations as well as its results in the operative.

3

Faithful to its title, the Martinist Order focuses mainly on studying and applying the original teaching of Louis-Claude de Saint-Martin and understanding the influence of his primary master, Martines de Pasqually, and of Jacob Bœhme, on his doctrine.[54]

---

52 *Martinezism, Willermozism, Martinism and Freemasonry* by Papus (Bayonne NJ: Rose Circle, 2020).

53 *L'Occultisme, esquisse d'un monde vivant* (Saint-Jean-de-la-Ruelle, Fr: Chanteloup, 1987).

54 "It is to Martines de Pasqually that I owe my entry into the higher truths. It is to Jacob Bœhme that I owe the most important steps I have taken in these truths." *Portrait,* No. 418 (Paris: Julliard, 1961).

First consequence: The Martinist Order is attached to the simplicity of the ritual forms, of which the primitive Martinist Order sets the example.

Second consequence: Fraternity and companionship are at the heart of the Martinist experience: "Do not be called Master. Because you have only one Master; and you are all brothers."[55]

Third consequence: A Martinist Order is as independent of any church as it is of any other initiatory order; members remain free to establish any compatible affiliations in the spirit. Equivalences between the ranks of the Martinist Order and those of other initiatory orders have existed. They are devoid of initiatory meaning.

Fourth consequence: The Martinist Order invites its members to embark on the path of Reintegration. This implies that it prepares them to free themselves from any form of alienation, including membership in any initiatory order including the Martinist Order.

---

55 Matt. 23:8.

IV—*Fraternity*

1

After the death of Papus, the Martinist Order branched out and the process did not stop. Any controversy between Martinist Orders concerning the precedence of one over the others is unseemly, provided that any order qualified as Martinist subscribes to the general principles set out above. Between the Martinist Orders as between the members of each Martinist Order, fraternity is the rule, and competition is admissible only in virtue.

2

All Martinist Orders providing the same initiation, a member of any Martinist Order can and must be received as a visitor in a meeting conducted under the auspices of another Martinist Order.

8 Three Narrow Doors

"Do not forget that there are two doors in the heart of Man; one, inferior, and by which the Enemy could be granted access to elementary light, and which may not be enjoyed except by this path; the other, superior, by which Man can give the Spirit captive with him access to the Divine Light that, here below, may only be communicated by this channel."

Louis-Claude de Saint-Martin

To approach Martinism as a way of awakening is to presuppose that the Martinist current, in its widest dimension and its operative expressions (through the Order of Knight Masons Elus Coëns of the Universe; the Rectified Scottish Rite, whose doctrine, it must be remembered, is Martinezism; the Martinist Order and the satellite orders that accompanied it and still accompany it today), present narrow, sometimes unsuspected, doors that the quester can open, sometimes even "accidentally," during his initiatory adventures.

Three of these doors will be explored here, without insistence. It is not a question of indicating precisely how to open doors that only ask to be hidden, but to illustrate how Martinism, in certain obscure recesses, or on the contrary in certain illuminated places, introduces to the ways of awakening.

We will take as a given the principle of Silence as the very foundation of initiation and as the source from which the way springs forth, whether it is internal or not. It is in the zone of Silence that these three doors can be opened. The first concerns the Order of Knight Masons Elus Coëns of the Universe, the second concerns the teaching of Master Philippe, and the third concerns the Rose-Croix, always in filigree, both as inspiration and as an ideal to be achieved, behind the operations of the Martinist Order.

The Order of Knight Masons Elus Coëns of the Universe

We refer the excellent works of Robert Amadou, Serge Caillet and Robert Ho-Than[56] to the reader who would not be familiar with the doctrine of *"the reintegration of beings into their first property, virtue, and divine spiritual power"* enacted by Martines de Pasqually, the doctrine which founds and frames the operations of Knight Masons Elus Coëns of the Universe, as the members of the priesthood of the Primitive Cult are referred to.

This order advocates the return to the central axis, our first condition, by a series of theurgic operations and alliances with the entities of successive circles that it is advisable to cross to return to the place that was ours before the fall, that is, the estrangement from the axis. The prototype of the theurgist is Seth. The reintegrated man regains his divine rank at the end of an ascension through the planetary spheres which correspond to certain psychic, energetic and essential stages.

In the West, the goals of the few initiatory orders which (at one time or another in their history and regardless of their current state) were truly operative and were vehicles of a real way, have roughly the same characteristics. They require of their members certain qualifications, martial (chivalrous), artistic, and priestly. In order to operate, it is necessary to access Silence at will and to remain there, to be capable of discipline, to have definitively renounced having and doing, to have approached the nature of

56 Book to be published.

nature, to be already familiar with Being, and to be inhabited by the presence of the Absolute.

Outside the zone of Silence, theurgy and alchemy are only posturing, stagecraft, even jokes, not always pleasant. The disciple, the one who practices the discipline, once initiated in the zone of Silence, has the choice between the non-way and the real ways. It is a very relative choice since it is determined by his nature and not by a reasoned choice. He can continue the divestments, continue to undo himself, until Being takes up all the space and carries him to the Absolute, which will dissolve all human reference within consciousness. It is a formidable direct way. He can explore and celebrate the Beauty, Strength, and Wisdom of Being through theurgy and alchemy.

The real ways begin with the connection to an eon-guide, regardless of the name and concept. From the conversation with the Holy Guardian Angel[57] to the tangible manifestation of an intermediary god, it is always an emanation of our own reality that would not exist if we were not there, any more than the scenery in which it manifests itself, the world or a world. The human being is populated with gods, archangels, angels, and an infinity of other entities that are so many self-conscious energies, more or less powerful, that gain autonomy as and when we disintegrate in the multiple. We are, ourselves, the Totality. The ten thousand beings, to use a Buddhist expression, live not only in us, but through us, in a very variable symbiosis according to the intensity of our own consciousness and our alignment with the Real.

This guiding entity, which can seemingly act as exfiltrated from our own body or manifest itself in a more internal way, always seemingly, according to two modes of reading, has a very

---

57 On this essential aspect of theurgy, read the introduction to *L'Anacrise pour avoir la communication avec son bon ange gardien*, published by Robert Amadou (Paris: Cariscript Publishing, 1988).

precise function, leading us to a series of arcana which contribute to the conquest of our own immortality, the establishment of our own divinity, the rejoining of our own reality.

Louis-Claude de Saint-Martin, after having realized with the system proposed by his first master, Martines de Pasqually, no longer wanted other mediators than Christ, who represents our solarity in its sovereign development. We will join him. Indeed, the fewer the intermediaries, logical levels, or representations that differ in order to approximate operational distinctions, the more we go to the simple, the more the influence of the One, unspeakable and immutable, is felt with power.

Often we have a magical vision of theurgy. Theurgy would make it possible, thanks to an alignment between intention, will, and orientation, to achieve one's own divinity. In many cases, however, theurgy seems to be more an action of the divine who celebrates himself out of all attachment, of all attainment, of any realization since "All is accomplished" has always been and always will be. The operator leaves room for the empty consciousness and frees all access to it, so that the divine can occupy it and accomplish what must be. In certain Gnostic currents, theurgy neither precedes nor accompanies alchemy, external or internal, but is reserved for those who, having realized the great work, are gods.

There is, in any case, a close relationship between theurgy and alchemy, either that one prepares or introduces to the other, or that they act simultaneously in a kind of coalition[58] the terms of which may be external or internal. External theurgy can be combined with metallic alchemy as with internal alchemy. It is the same for an internal theurgy such as that which Louis-Claude de Saint-Martin was finally able to implement. Whatever the approach, the transition to the internal is required when dualistic perception fades. Theurgy and alchemy are like two phases of the same breath.

---

58   From the Latin *coalescere,* "to unite."

Neither Martines de Pasqually nor Louis-Claude de Saint-Martin were alchemists. But any theurgy can convey an alchemy: the Holy Mass is a brilliant demonstration of it. Some have tried in the past to give an interpretation of Martinezist doctrine in the field of metallic alchemy. This attempt, though intellectually interesting, was not operatively conclusive.

More relevant seems the interpretation of the doctrine of the reintegration of beings in the field of internal alchemy, as suggested by the study of the twenty philosophical paintings published by Robert and Catherine Amadou in the *Angéliques*.[59]

These twenty paintings that were to be part of a series with many more, since some bear numbers going beyond 20, up to 39, illustrate the different stages of reintegration as it is carried out by the operations of the Elus Coëns. Many of the paintings depict, among other elements that evolve in the circles of manifestation, the serpentine powers without which anything can be done.

The serpentine powers that weave the web of time and worldly experience must be identified, remembered, oriented towards the kingdom of the center, reintegrated in the axis, and verticalized in the deification of the human being, in the realization of a body of glory, in the conquest of immortality, in the ultimate liberation.

It is not useful here to write a treatise on the serpentine powers, or "draconic" powers at work in both alchemy and theurgy, but to bring the reader to study the meaning of these philosophical images under the aspect of internal alchemy.

Thus Plate 5[60] and Plate 8[61]: (following pages)

---

59 *Angéliques*, Volume I, Catherine and Robert Amadou, *Première édition intégrale d'après les manuscrits de Louis-Claude de Saint-Martin* (Guérigny, Fr: CIREM, 2001).

60 *Angéliques*, Volume I, page 224. Drawing reworked from the published *Angéliques* for better visibility.

61 *Angéliques*, Volume I, page 225. Drawing reworked from the published *Angéliques* for better visibility.

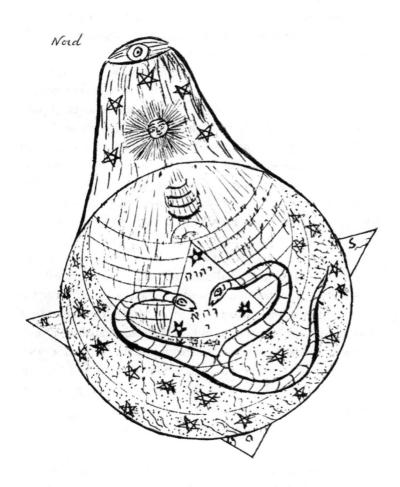

Plate 5

Plate 8

The figures speak volumes. Certain drawings by Louis-Claude de Saint-Martin seem to indicate that he knew the lesser philosophical *arcanum* and the great sacerdotal *arcanum* (which, in alchemical symbolism, are also called the "wet principle" and the "igneous principle") and their implementation in internal alchemy. Put in a certain order, which is up to the reader to determine, the philosophical figures that have come down to us convey the lesser *arcanum* and the great *arcanum* as well as their implementation. It is probable that it is by the play of correspondences and not by a deliberate intention that an internal alchemy is thus found coded in these images.

This can illustrate the fact that as we approach the center and the conditions fade away, the "absolute structure" that Raymond Abellio[62] has modeled brilliantly for us is so significant that it stands out in all the forms that literally coincide, that is, "fall together,"[63] leaving the Real bare.

Master Philippe of Lyon

Master Philippe of Lyon, whose real name is Nizier Anthelme Philippe (1849-1905), remains a mystery. The closer we get to it, the more the mystery grows. However, today we have the opportunity to get to know him better thanks to the numerous testimonies published by the editor Geneviève Dubois[64] which thus largely contributed to the renewal of interest in the thought, the testimony, and the work of Master Philippe which until then had hardly concerned anything other than a small number of Marti-

---

62   *La structure absolue* by Raymond Abellio (Paris: Gallimard, NRF, 1965).

63   From the scholastic Latin *coincĭdere.*

64   See the collection of books *Autour du Maître Philippe* from Editions Le Mercure Dauphinois and the excellent film, available on DVD, titled *Maître Philippe de Lyon, le chien du berger,* also from Mercure Dauphinois, 2007.

nists and a few heirs to the Lyon tradition.

These publications, to which must be added the research work of Serge Caillet,[65] should make it possible to free up the teaching of Master Philippe from the impact of the narrow-mindedness that had appropriated it, to restore all its radiance. Indeed, as much of the teaching of Master Philippe constitutes an opening, so the "Philippines," as Robert Amadou called them, worked to reduce it to a superstitious devotion, to such an extent that many Martinists mistrust the Lyonnais master by rejection of those who claim it, even today, very badly.

The question, constantly posed, "Who is Master Philippe?" has never found a satisfactory answer. We will not settle it. It is enough to know that Philippe was an astonishing miracle worker who masterfully demonstrated that the Universe is a responsive structure, a master of the Art who knew how to operate in the laboratory to develop effective medicines intended for his many patients and who was, undoubtedly, an awakener. François Trojani perfectly noted what distinguishes Master Philippe:

> There have always manifested particularly gifted beings outside of initiation.
>
> Without trying to establish a primacy or a hierarchy between them, what is however remarkable, even almost unique here, is the extent and the quality of the powers manifested by this being. For years I have carefully verified the authenticity of the facts reported. I have compared him with other men endowed with powers and I must say that his remain an enigma defying reason. Asceticism, even holiness. No doubt because they are of the order of Faith, Grace, or Mystery.
>
> The conclusion I have drawn from this is that there are pow-

65 *Monsieur Philippe «l'Ami de Dieu»* by Serge Caillet (Paris: Dervy, 2013).

ers of an infinitely higher order, acting through simple, everyday words, with humility and love as the center. But we are here a thousand leagues from litanies, Gods, magic, and knowledge, and this path is undoubtedly not suitable for everyone.[66]

What is striking about Philippe is indeed the simplicity, which borders on banality, of his words. Certainly, in duality, only banalities can appear as truths, but it is a matter of something quite different from common sense.

Let's take a few words attributed to Master Philippe:

> If you want Heaven to hear your prayers, love your neighbor as yourself, do not hold grudges against anyone, never speak of the absent. Thirsty people are those who in this time or another have drunk when they were not thirsty. When you give alms, do it in the shadows and without expecting a reward from heaven, because if you have this thought, you are paying yourself. But give alms with kindness as a thing due to a brother.[67]

"To love one another" in the dual experience becomes, through the action of the archaic triangle of power—territory—reproduction, "to love some more than others" or "to love some and not to love others," "to love the ones against the others" or even "to love oneself against all others." Michel de Roisin, in a fascinating book devoted to the Ekklesia Kataugue[68] (it is still not known to date whether it had an existence elsewhere than in the mind of that author), noted that man does not love himself, whereas the Ek-

---

66 *Le Maître Philippe de Lyon* by Francois Trojani in *L'Originel n° 2, Les sociétés secrètes d'Occident* (Paris: 1995).

67 *Monsieur Philippe « l'Ami de Dieu »* by Serge Caillet (Paris,: Dervy, 2013), pp. 309-310, quoted from the *Journal de séances*.

68 *Ulrich de Mayence (1485-1558), la Bible de l'An 2000, le Maître de Nostradamus* by Michel de Roisin (Monoco: Rocher, 1997).

klesia Kataugue invited one to "love others even more than one-self." In all these cases, the human being is caught in the net of comparison, memory, and personal history.

No religion committed so many crimes as Christianity, which taught that one should love others as oneself. The failure is obvious, and it was inevitable, because reason, fueled by faith, is powerless to fight *en masse* against the conditioning of the species. If there is another, sooner or later, it is experienced as an element of comparison and nourishes desire. If there is desire, there is need and lack. If there is a lack, there is risk and risk of escalation.

The spiritual counsel of Master Philippe, "To love your neighbor as yourself," involves two prerequisites that were known to the regulars of the Temple of Delphi. The famous "Know thyself..." and the less known, but equally important, "Take care of yourself." Loving one's own ego, one's "person," generates dominant and dominated relationships with one's peers. Philippe therefore invites you to love your own reality, your own divinity, and to recognize yourself as such. Once your original, divine nature has been recognized, it is advisable to take care of it, not to alter or disturb it. The word "mental" is synonymous with "disorder." Philip, in his teaching, never ceases to invite Silence, to silence envy, greed, jealousy, and pride that arise from desire.

Henceforth, there is no more charity nor gift, which presuppose a separation and a more or less repressed expectation on both sides, a need for recognition, a need for belonging. It is only in nondual experience that Love can blossom. In the dualistic world, love appears as a bridge thrown desperately over one's sense of separation and abandonment.

Whoever recognizes his divine nature recognizes it at the same time in all that lives and in this "other," mirror of himself. Then, in the intimacy of the nondual experience, it is possible and even inevitable to love the other as oneself because, here and now, in this parenthesis of the Real, there is neither "me" nor "other," but only Being. And when Master Philippe invites us to become, like him, "very small," it is not a matter of the false humility of the self, but of our capacity for emptiness and silence, for nothing, of our capacity to become a receptacle to welcome Being in its radiance and absoluteness.

On the other hand, the "neighbor" is not the "similar," the neighbor is "the one who comes,"[69] "the one who approaches,"[70] is also the friend, the intimate, the neighbor of the One in the language of the birds, this New Man who we must accept and welcome as a new self rather than resist for fear of change and distrust of the unknown, the One-known.

> If you stayed only half a day without having bad thoughts, bad words, without talking about the absent, without judging any-one, the prayer you would say afterwards would be heard from Heaven.[71]

Of course, even in the first degree, this injunction is not unneces-sary. In Masonic and esoteric circles (and Martinism is no excep-tion), there are more peddlers of gossip and unfounded rumors than initiates, including some among the leaders. Here we see the effect of the intrusion of the profane person into the bosom

---

69 Which can evoke, on the axis of temporality, "the race that comes," from the novel *The Coming Race* (Edinburgh, London: Black-wood, 1871) by Bulwer-Lytton, famous author of *Zanoni, A Rosicrucian Tale,* and, on the axis of transcendence, the New Man of Louis-Claude de Saint-Martin.

70 On this subject, read *Le Grand Œuvre comme fondement d'une spir-itualité laïque. Le chemin vers l'Individuation* by Claude Bruley (Cordes sur Ciel, Fr: Rafael de Surtis, 2008).

71 *Monsieur Philippe « l'Ami de Dieu »* by Serge Caillet (Paris: Dervy, 2013), p. 310, quoted from the *Journal de séances.*

of the sacred person, an intrusion made possible by the absence of initiatory practices and spiritual disciplines.

On another level, the energetic, the altered state of consciousness that indulges in these behaviors, which have unfortunately become common in all circles, is marked by the presence of what Helena Roerich calls "imperil." Imperil is an energetic poison that coagulates and becomes a brake, if not an obstacle, to the work of clarification and fluidity that the initiate must lead. The imperil thickens, opacifies, and freezes the initiatory process. Only the work of disidentification from the person makes it possible to free oneself from the powerful imprint of the archaic triangle. It is obviously the power struggles, the turf wars, and the hypertrophy of the need for replication that originate these drifts. These should not be confused with initiatory transgressions or perfectly controlled provocations intended to break the shackles of prejudices and presuppositions that enclose being. Such liberating transgressions are the prerogative of consciousnesses not identified with a reducing ego. They are characterized by elegance. Such transgressions do not hurt, they surprise, shift, and ultimately illuminate.

Only the technical work of self-remembering which makes it possible to slow down and stop the internal dialogue can introduce a state of non-thought out of which thought is the plaything of conditioning. "Pure is he who is without thought," says the hermetic adage. Outside of silence, thought is caught up in personal identifications and conditioning that are organized into comparisons, evaluations, and judgments.

"Having good thoughts," as opposed to "having bad thoughts," nurtures duality and nourishes antagonisms. It also often establishes as absolute truth a very relative statement and, very logically, marginalizes, condemns, and excludes. "Do not judge" is only possible in Silence.

These two examples show the very deep, direct, and spiritually revolutionary impact of these simple words, words that lead to the Simple, the One.

But there are still other powers of the mind, other divine astonishments in the words of Nizier Anthelme Philippe:

> *Diamonds:* the diamond differs from other similar stones in that it has received something from above.
>
> They are only objects, a kind of concretion that formed in the saliva of certain dragons, of which we still find skeletons nine yards long. They disappeared and the diamonds remained, but they will die too; the total lifespan of a diamond does not exceed 15,000 or 16,000 years. There are already old diamonds on the verge of dying, they are softening: these are the yellows. Large diamonds are still found, but very few; there are no mines, since the diamond is individual; it is an insect. What led to the belief in the existence of diamond mines is that if in a land there are several diamonds, they tend to come together little by little. We will arrive at the artificial manufacture of diamonds, but we must first find this truth: that the diamond comes from the serpent.
>
> It is with Lachesis that the diamond will be made, or rather Lachesis is one of the virtues of which the diamond is the opposite pole.

This passage is from the *Recueil de Papus,*[72] a collection of talks from his guide, rated and listed by theme. The words of Master Philippe on diamonds were classified by Papus, with great relevance, under the heading "Alchemy." Reading the remarks of Master Philippe concerning diamonds is perplexing. Is it a fairy tale for children? Isn't the decryption of alchemical texts just

---

72 *Monsieur Philippe « l'Ami de Dieu »* by Serge Caillet (Paris: Dervy, 2013), pp. 264-265, quoted from the *Journal de séances.*

considered child's play? The freshness and liveliness of a childlike spirit are indeed necessary to identify the puns, allusions, and improbable links that multiply in alchemical fables.

If the adamantine words of Master Philippe are not "empty words," as they will appear to the uninformed reader, they will interest to a high degree the reader familiar with internal alchemy. Internal pathways are sometimes referred to as "adamantines." The diamond formed from the dragon's saliva refers precisely to a practice of internal alchemy on the so-called ways of immortality, both Western and Eastern. The phrase "the diamond comes from the snake" further reinforces the specificity of the subject, again indicating a particular operativity of the internal channels. Added to this is the reference to Lachesis. This snake belongs to the genus *crotalinae.* One of the species is called the "mute rattlesnake." He lives hidden, isolated from human presence, like the adept devoted to internal alchemy. Its venom has the particularity of breaking down the blood and making it more fluid, which is why it is used as a remedy. In internal alchemy, it is common that the remedy is a poison that kills the "person" identified with the dream of the world, but frees the being when it is absorbed in an objective state.

Finally, we will remember that Lachesis, the fateful, is the Fate[73] who puts the thread on the spindle while Clotho will spin it and Atropos, the inflexible, will cut it when the time comes, at the fixed hour. The conditioned human being cannot escape his destiny. But the initiate, who knows how to turn poison into a divine elixir, is no longer affected by fate, but elected. The word *lachesis* means in Greek "lot" or "act of drawing lots," which evokes the real election that is traditionally done by drawing lots and not by a vote.

---

73 The Three Fates are daughters of Jupiter and Themis, the goddess of Justice. They determine and regulate the fate of humans. Lachesis measures the time allotted to each one.

The teaching of Master Philippe is perhaps not an obsolete morality. It is part of a kingdom where duality is absent, where the One reigns. His word, issued from Silence, is a creative Word if it is received in Silence, a Word that feeds the embryo of immortality or divinity that we carry within us.

> Space is not empty, but full. The planes of the elementals are within us. Heaven is also in us—it is we who are not in Heaven. Everything is in us. We are as if in an embryonic state.[74]

The Rose-Croix

Master Philippe did not have a high opinion of the Rose-Croix. This is because he hardly knew anything other than the colorful episode of "the war of the two roses" which opposed Joséphin Péladan and Stanislas de Guaïta.

Martinism was and remains in its contemporary expression, that is to say since Papus, associated with Rosicrucian expressions, and particularly with the Kabbalistic Order of the Rose-Croix.[75]

But these are not forms borrowed from the Tradition that we are going to talk about here, but of its poetic and metaphysical essence which the Rose-Croix wonderfully expresses.

We will start from a schema that I proposed to Robert Amadou in 2002 to study the distinction between Réau-Croix and Rose-Croix, or between two approaches to the Real.

---

74 *Monsieur Philippe « l'Ami de Dieu »* by Serge Caillet (Paris: Dervy, 2013), p. 300, quoted from the *Journal de séances*.

75 Robert Amadou and the author restored the Kabbalistic Order of the Rose-Croix in 1997, as in 1992 they had organized the second resurgence of the Order of Knight Masons Elus Coëns of the Universe.

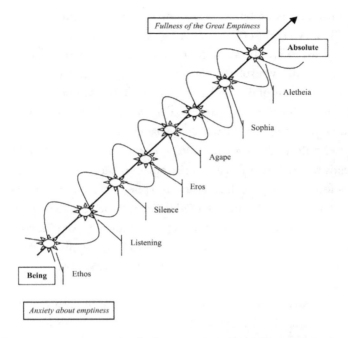

The initiatory process leads the consciousness of our original nature, Being, to our ultimate nature, the Absolute. The memory of our original nature is translated by an experience, the anxiety about emptiness, which sets us in motion, from an unbearable stillness to a divine stillness. The realization of our Being in the Absolute is an imperience,[76] the fullness of the Great Emptiness or the Great Real.

There are as many schemas as there are individuals. It is possible, however, to draw trends, and those represented by the two magnificent expressions of "Réau-Croix"[77] and "Rose-Croix" con-

76 [Trans.] Imperience: the content of embodied consciousness unmediated by thought, language, or memory. Experience is what we retain from our imperiences.

77 Last rank of the scale of the Order of Knight Masons Elus Coëns of the Universe. The word Réau-Croix, like the word Rose-Croix, designates a state of consciousness freed from all limits.

stitute two major tendencies found in all the traditional currents.

The two paths of the Réau-Croix and the Rose-Croix intersect in necessary (in the sense of inevitable) knots, on the axis of the Real, in our own solarity. Among these nodes, or crossroads between the axis of having and doing and the axis of being, we noted: *ethos, listening, silence, eros* and *agape, sophia, aletheia.*[78] Others could fit in this list. We will come back to it.

The Réau-Croix, or rather the one who takes the path that leads to the state of Réau-Croix, borrows the schema of respect for forms, to acquire the method and release the energies that will lead him to the Essence, the *Eidos.* For this, he goes through each circle of the manifestation (or representation) before moving on to the more immediate inner circle until he gradually reaches the "Center of the Centers." The word "réau" evokes the wheel, the circle.

The Rose-Croix, the one who is part of the path that leads to the state of Rose-Croix, starts from Essence, or more exactly, from the feeling that he has of it, in order to ally himself with energies to illuminate the forms. The method of the Rose-Croix is freedom, which requires a great deal of discipline. Rather than go through all the peripheries, once the circularity of the experience has been clearly identified, he uses an arc to move back to the center. The word "rose" evokes the heart, the center.

We can illustrate both approaches in the field of meditation. The Réau-Croix receives a form of meditation. He respects it, practices it, integrates it, makes it a method, even an art, and gradually gives life to the meditator in the play of conscience and energy. The Rose-Croix sees—because he knows, he is "born with it"—that the meditator is already in him. He goes in search of him

---

78 The use of Greek words is only intended to lead us to question ourselves about the experience that gives meaning, to force us to move from the surface structure of the experience to its deep structure.

by removing everything that is not him. The Réau-Croix meditates. The Rose-Croix lets God meditate in him.

Both therefore go through energy knots that need to be untied. The knot freezes the energy in temporality. These passages, the true initiations, can occur in a different order from one path to another and even from one individual to another. However, they all seem to start with *ethos* and end with the sequence *Sophia—Aletheia* before the final shift into the Great Real.

Ethos is not ethics in the usual sense of the term, although used today very improperly in many situations. *Ethos* is the character, the habitual way of being, or rather of not being, that is to say the relational complex of conditionings and heterogeneous identifications that constitute the "person." The *ethos* underlies the study of this complex, the *"pragmateia,"* a manner to which we will not return. It is indispensable. In the Rose-Croix, it is accompanied by an aesthetic. This praxis of Silence requires special Listening, making all the senses available to what presents itself, which includes the senses of perception, the senses of action, the internal sense of "I," the mind, and the intellect. This letting go makes it possible to fully experience Eros and Agape, without which experimentation, the Sophianic coronation could only be ephemeral and would be transformed, taken up by the egoic game, into a new veil thrown over *aletheia,* the truth, not the spoken truth, the *veritas* resulting from discourse, but the unveiling of Being.

Other nodes can be part of this schema, in particular that of *tekhnè* (discussed earlier) to be appropriated, which is interesting to consider in the opposition between *praxis* and *poiesis. Praxis,* the Greek word for action, designates the operativities in our fields. *Praxis* is an action that is self-sufficient, a celebration that seeks no external realization, production, or work. *Poiesis,* on the contrary, seeks *ergon,* outer work.

Ergon or *parergon,* here is an apparent distinction between the way of the Réau-Croix and the way of the Rose-Croix. The initial formulation of the way of the Réau-Croix is undoubtedly more dualistic than that of the way of the Rose-Croix which, as a preliminary, insists on the elusive character of the Spirit and thus places itself in a nondual perspective. But this distinction is only valid for the first steps. The reassuring dualist framework of the Elus Coëns joins in Silence the delicious uncertainty of the Rose-Croix as to form. Practice, in any case, dissolves the dualistic character of representation, confuses the object and the subject before rendering them to nothing. If the Real were dual, the Great Work, whether theurgic or alchemical, could be accomplished externally without requiring an internal transmutation, which is radically denied by imperience.

Following the observation of this schema, Robert Amadou made several remarks quite relevant to the subject at hand. He first noted that the schema could be read in two directions, descending and ascending, and that the stages, nodes, and intermediate states bore a Gnostic mark. He drew a parallel with the Valentinian system or even the Universal Figure of Martines de Pasqually, which he said "nevertheless specializes in the Réau-Croix current." And he posed the question of where to include the path of Louis-Claude de Saint-Martin which is obviously not that of the Réau-Croix, but neither that of the Rose-Croix because "its operativity and technique are entirely internal"? Robert Amadou then referred to the Society of Independents,[79] whose powers certainly recall those of the Rose-Croix. He suggested that the disciples of Louis-Claude de Saint-Martin should be qualified par excellence as "Independents," recognizing that they would nevertheless skip the major stages of *ethos, listening, silence, eros* and *agape, sophia, aletheia,* but attain anyway!

79 See *Le Crocodile ou la guerre du bien et du mal* (Paris: Triades, 1962).

9   Reintegration According to the Rectified Scottish Rite

"You ought to conceive equally the possibility of the darkness which poured upon the spirit of Man because of the deeds which he did against the Law of the Creator; for as soon as he, without regard to his glorious rank as a pure spiritual creature, had conceived and executed the monstrous project of nourishing himself with material fruits, as the traditions have declared, he did not hesitate to regard himself as a material being."

Excerpts from the instruction of the Professed Knight, p. 4

I WOULD LIKE TO FOCUS, in a non-exhaustive way, on three aspects of this passage of the instruction, that of the doctrine of the Reintegration of Beings, that of the Solomonic doctrine that elegantly permeates the Rectified Scottish Rite[80] (RER),[81] and that of the nondual metaphysics to which, ultimately, all traditions point, even those of dualistic expression.

In this passage, Jean Baptiste Willermoz refers to the second fall according to the doctrine of Reintegration, a theme that he

---

80   We refer the reader to an in-depth study of the Reintegration doctrine within the Rectified Scottish Rite in our work, *The Rectified Scottish Rite: From the Doctrine of Reintegration to the* Imago Templi, with prefaces by Serge Caillet and José Anes (Bayonne, NJ: Rose Circle, forthcoming 2022).

81   RER: (French) *Régime Écossais Rectifié,* the Rectified Scottish Rite.

takes up in the instructions intended for the Professed Knight and Grand Professed Knight as well as in other writings, especially in Books D1 through D9 in the G. Kloss collection.

Let us first recall the process of the double fall. God has always emanated the free beings or spirits who constitute His court, His celestial assembly. Some of them rebel against their Creator. Whatever the metaphysical meaning of this rebellion, it is also turns out to be toxic for the spirits who remained faithful to the Lord, which leads God to isolate the rebellious spirits in the material world created for this purpose. Adam is a singular spirit, member of a class of beings emanated from God in His likeness, that of man, to guard the material world, but also "to educate the demons" who inhabit it. Adam failed in his mission on the day when, fascinated by the prince of the fallen spirits, he tried to father a creature, Eve—a mistake. Eve is endowed with a body of darkness. Adam thus lost his body of light and took, like Eve, a dark body that kept him prisoner of matter. The jailer became a prisoner of the world he had been chosen to rule. This dramatic process can be interpreted in different ways, all of which have operative consequences. Let us remember for the moment that Adam and ourselves, who are his descendants, can no longer escape from the temporality, the causality, the separation that typifies duality, the darkness according to Willermoz.

Ceremonial magic or theurgy is imposed on us, according to Martines de Pasqually, because, since this second fall, we are incapable of spiritual operations. In a Spinozist mode, we could say that we can no longer intervene at the level of the first kind of knowledge, that of perceptions or forms, and only occasionally at the level of the second kind of knowledge, that of causes, but are mostly confined to the level of the third kind of knowledge, that of essences. The question that arises for us, which tends to extract us from the darkness is: what operativity replaces theurgy within the RER? Beneficence, yes, but what do we mean by that? Societal beneficence does not require an initiatory order and methodology, so it is a spiritual and metaphysical beneficence that we must discover and implement in its different forms. The Hebrew word *teshuvah* means the return to the previous state and evokes reintegration, but the *shuv* root of this word means "good." "To do well" is to reintegrate and reintegrate oneself, to return to our original and ultimate state, in permanent reality, "That which remains."

Several Hebrew and Greek words from the Old Testament and New Testament, carrying nuances, are translated into French by the same words, "the darkness(es)" or "the abyss." In Genesis 1:2, there is talk of "darkness over the face of the abyss." This trilogy of terms is interesting, especially the middle word "face." With the second fall, we lose the face-to-face with God, returning to the darkness of matter, taking the risk of the destructive abyss, the Hebrew *tehom*. The Hebrew words translated "fall" in the Bible carry more the meaning of exile than of fall. Note then that historical time, *Chronos,* is eternity in exile.

Man is the recapitulation of creation. Since the second fall, God has constituted Himself as a Temple in the bosom of the world, that is to say, in the bosom of Man. Darkness is the "external" light, the light of the world, dualistic, which, in the eyes of the original and ultimate divine light, is only darkness. By the principle of the devil,[82] *diabolos,* never so named in the doctrine of Reintegration, the divine separates, in the appearance, the One from the multiple, the uncreated from the created. This is the fragmentation and the suffering that accompanies it. The Hydra of Herne symbolizes this duality when each severed head gives

---

82 It is necessary to distinguish the ontological Satan from the separating Satan, the devil. See the remarkable work of Annick de Souzenelle, *Le Seigneur et le Satan* (Paris: Albin Michel, 2016).

birth to two new heads.

Jean-Baptiste Willermoz brings together the two doctrines, the doctrine of Reintegration and the doctrine of Solomon's Temple in the rank of Apprentice. But the fertile play of mirrors between the two only develops fully and masterfully in the degree of Scottish Master of Saint Andrew. A double reading, phanic (what God shows) and critical (what God veils) is necessary to discover the praxis inscribed in the mythemes, these compounds of myths.

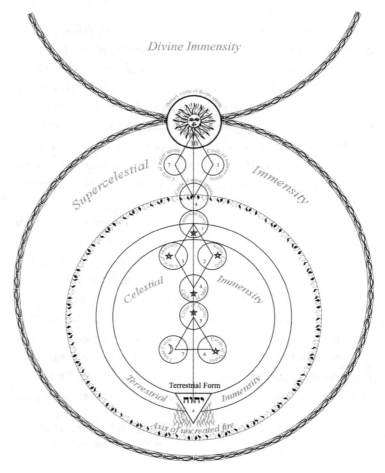

At this grade, we are indeed offered the path of Reintegration, both in the east and on the breasts of the Brothers, by the hexagram pointed at its center, and the reconstruction of the Temple of Solomon, by the ritual. This degree is also the place-state where the quester escapes the ternary replication and renews the alliance lost since the fall with the 4. Louis-Claude de Saint-Martin explains:[83]

> Explanation of the numbers 4 and 3, which constitute the two natures of man in his present state; the number 4 being attributed to his spiritual soul and the number 3 being that of the principles that make up his bodily form. The first, giving us 10 by its addition to itself [1+2+3+4=10], presents to us the image of the unity from which it emanates and thereby announces to us that its essence is eternal, since it is the same as that of God; the second, not being a unity and having no center or anything of its own, indicates to us that it is an assembly which has begun and which must end. (...)
>
> In the end, the link that binds them to each other must be broken and they must continue to move away until the perfect reintegration of each one at its source, namely the particular bodies in the general body, the general body in the central fire axis and the spiritual soul of man in his divine principle.

No one can reintegrate the Holy City or heavenly Jerusalem if he has not rebuilt or liberated, according to the operative approach, this body of glory. This integration is present at the degree of Scottish Master of Saint Andrew in the hexagram, the double triangle of the East or Seal of Solomon which brings together the four symbols of Water, Air, Fire, and Earth into one. At its center, the letter H represents not only Hiram, but Hély, to be dis-

---

83 *Les Leçons de Lyon aux élus coëns,* op. cit., lesson of Wednesday, March 6, 1776 (Paris: Dervy, 1999).

tinguished from the prophet Elijah, or, according to Martines de Pasqually, the Rhély, mysterious figure of Christ, the only indispensable mediator, spirit of God who animates all the Prophets, including the "historical" Christ, fully and absolutely, Wisdom being the feminine aspect of Rhély.

In the symbolic environment proposed by the decor of the degree of Scottish Master of Saint Andrew we discover another version of the Universal Figure of Martines de Pasqually. We find in fact the seven planets of the universal figure in another arrangement: Saturn in the center (natural habitat of Adam, which was excluded during the second fall) a Moon—Mercury—Sun triangle, and a Mars—Venus—Jupiter triangle. The observer is on Earth. In front of him are several possible ways to get closer to the center, inaccessible without the intervention of Christ or the Holy Spirit of Christ, Hély, or Rhély.

If theurgy, for which Martines de Pasqually is (for want of a better expression) calling, is removed, what praxis does Jean-Baptiste Willermoz invite us to implement? It is, of course, impossible to distinguish what belongs to his conscious intention from what the multiplicity of symbols entails. Whatever the approach, we must remember that praxis is indispensable. All theory, all doctrine, leads to the external through comparison and analytic treatment which necessarily fragment, while praxis leads to the internal. Let's see what the rituals of the Rectified Scottish Rite can tell us.

We must, I believe, remember the three temples of Solomon: the Temple of stone,[84] the Temple of paper, and the Temple of man. In 586 BC, the first temple of Solomon, a stone temple, was destroyed by Nebuchadnezzar. This is the Babylonian exile, for 70 years according to the Jewish tradition, until the Persian victory over the Babylonians. Freed, the Jews return to Judea and rebuild the Temple.

In 70 AD, Vespasian, then a Roman general, surrounded Jerusalem with his troops. The besieged city is close to defeat when a chief rabbi, Yohanan Ben Zakkai, escapes from the city, joins General Vespasian's encampment, introduces himself and salutes him by bowing to him as Emperor. While Vespasian, offended, is about to punish him, a messenger, just arrived from Rome, announces to him that he has just been named Emperor. Impressed by the rabbi's foreknowledge, Vespasian asks him what he wants.

---

84 Note that in the second Temple of stone, there was no golden Ark as in the first. The High Priest had to visualize it in his mind. In place of the Ark was just a foundation stone. This detail can be considered as an announcement of the dematerialization and progressive spiritualization of the Temple. The dimensions of this foundation stone are 52.3 (cubits) by 32.4 × 32.4 according to the traditions of the Brotherhood. We find these dimensions in the perspective of the Ark of the Covenant in Chartres Cathedral.

Instead of demanding the end of the siege and the protection of Solomon's Temple, Ben Zakkai asked him for permission to found with a few disciples a Talmudic school in a small town, Yavne. Vespasian agrees, somewhat surprised by this unexpected request. This event is considered to be the founding of Judaism.[85] This school will produce a remarkable teaching: Mishnah, midrash, gematria, Zohar, Kabbalah, philosophy, wisdom texts, poetry, Jewish literature, etc., a culture of paper succeeding the culture of stone. The invisible temple of paper supplants the temple of stone which will again be destroyed and heralds an even more elusive temple, the Temple of the Spirit,[86] Inner temple, Temple of man and Temple in man to be paralleled by the primitive Cult of the doctrine of Reintegration, the prototype of all cults.

This Temple of Man is traditionally made up of four "places" that correspond to the structure of the spiritual body of Man, as to the "body" of God. It is not wrong to make a link, without comparison however, between these four parts of the Temple and the four immensities of the doctrine of Reintegration (divine immensity, supercelestial immensity, celestial immensity, and terrestrial immensity). These four places of the Temple, which are also the four "times," *Chronos, Aion, Kairos,* and Eternity, are the Court of the Women, the *Azarah* (which hosted the sacrifices), the *Ulam* (the sanctuary), and the *Holy of Holies.* Each of the chambers of Solomon's Temple can be related to a spiritual organ of the Body

---

85 *Jérusalem, trois fois sainte* by Marc-Alain Ouaknin, Philippe Markiewicz, Mohammed Taleb, *Arpenter le sacré* collection (Paris: Desclée de Brouwer, 2016).

86 And back to the prototype, the *Imago Templi.* Indeed, in Exodus 25:9 and 25:40, it is given to Moses to contemplate the *Imago Templi* for inspiration: "And see to it that you make them according to the pattern which was shown you on the mountain." (Exodus 25:40). It seems, however, that rather than a vision, it is a hearing that is at stake. God speaks to Moses, who does not see, and dictates to him His instructions.

of Glory. More generally, the head evokes the *Holy of Holies,* the trunk corresponds to the sanctuary, the sexual organs to the *Ulam,* the feet resting on the court.

Within the Temple of Man,[87] we reach the *Ulam* (Abdomen) from the court by the feet (Earth). We enter the sanctuary (rib-cage) after the action of the sexual organs and kidneys (Water). We reach the Holy of Holies (skull) through the ear and the mouth (Air), the mouth and the ear being symbolically equivalents of the female sex. At the top of the skull is access to the Absolute (Fire). Here we are in the presence of an internal alchemy, analogous moreover in principle to that of Cagliostro and his Egyptian High Masonry.[88] Three alchemical fires are at work: sexual fire, bile fire, and salivary fire, for a total integration by fire as a principle. If, according to Martines de Pasqually, air is rarefied water, this process of rarefaction then invites us to reach this salutary principal Fire, to the death of the breath. Now in Hebrew, the letters of the word *Ruach,* often translated as Breath, *Ruach,* Spirit or Holy Spirit, pronounced slightly differently, *Rewah,* signifies the interval, the access to the divine within the same duality, the light even in the bosom of darkness.

Note that it is indeed from the flesh and not against the flesh that this temple of the Spirit is built or brought to light. In the second fall, Adam turns around. His interior becomes exterior and *Basar,* his essential flesh, of the nature of the Spirit, is constituted as flesh, the outer shell. There is therefore a continuum from the flesh to the Spirit, the flesh being carried back to its true nature by the process of Reintegration. The Hebrew expression

---

87 For a more subtle division taking into account the organs of the human body in correspondence with the Temple, see *The Rectified Scottish Rite: From the Doctrine of Reintegration to the* Imago Templi by Rémi Boyer (Bayonne, NJ: Rose Circle, forthcoming 2022).

88 Or more generally to the principle of internal alchemy whether called Oriental or Occidental.

Kol Basar means "all flesh" as well as "all soul" and in the Book of Job we read "From my flesh I will see Eloah," that is, God.

Another indication can lead us towards an internal alchemy. The Lodge, in the RER, meets in the forecourt. The Lodge table reflects the columns, inverted; the luminaries, the Sun and the Moon. It is therefore a mirror. On the forecourt, the only object that can act as a mirror is the Brazen Sea. It was standing in the southeastern corner of the inner courtyard (1 Kings 7:39; 2 Chr. 4:10). A Jewish tradition teaches us that this basin was melted by the bronzier Hiram from the mirrors given to the Temple by the women for its manufacture. We thus move from a horizontal mirror in which the masks, the "persons," the egos, are reflected in an ascending mirror that re-establishes the relationship between the earth and the sky, between "the waters below" and "the waters above." It is in front of this Brazen Sea that the recipient of the degree of Scottish Master of Saint Andrew will find himself, the degree where he is also confronted with another mirror that restores the face-to-face with God, namely, the Golden Delta allegedly worn by Master Hiram, discovered by the architect Jabulum during the excavations carried out on the site of the Temple for its reconstruction. This delta presents the sacred name on one side while the other side is a mirror.

Let's continue with the brass. For Isaiah (60:17), brass is intermediate between wood and gold, between nature and Light. Another object, the brass serpent of Moses, which restores life, interests us here. The serpent is called *Nechesh* in Hebrew, *Nun, Chet, Shin*, the fish, the barrier, the divine fire. It is the serpent that, at each stage, evaluates the capacity to move to the next chamber of the body in this verticality which is also a path of reintegration. Let us observe the kinship between *Nechesh*, the serpent and *Nechoshet*, the bronze. The brass serpent of Moses, which destroys the serpents of the Egyptian magi, is a serpent of serpents, vertical, which redirects the energy of the serpentine powers that weave horizontal peripheral realities. This evokes the "coiled," the energy located at the base of the spine to which it is advisable to give back its ascending freedom by directing it to the "Higher Sense."

This serpentine power, reoriented in verticality, becomes *Yod,* which is also Christ. God extracted from Adam his feminine, Eve, so that he may become aware of her, marry her, and make her fruitful. It is a matter of remembering this part of himself, Eve, identified with the archaic triangle of power—territory—reproduction that supports the duality of the created, Eve, his *Ishah,* to better reintegrate her by fertilizing her luminously. In the Here and Now, the *Kairos,* Adam enters the created, Eve, the unfulfilled, transmits to her the divine seed in the alchemical marriage of mating. He reintegrates *Ishah* within himself to achieve divine unity. When Adam turns away from the divinity, from his own divinity as well, he fertilizes Eve with a toxic, dark substance that disintegrates, crumbles, multiplies duality, and darkens. In *Kairos,* Adam fertilizes *Ishah* as Christ, as God. Out of Here and Now, Adam fertilizes *Ishah* as Satan, the separator. Note that a Hebrew anagram of Adam is the *Me'od,* the quality of Spirit in Man, but also, the desire that the human being has for God.[89] Adam, by uniting with Lilith, remains unfinished because Lilith represents pleasure without love. Completion is possible only with Lilith who has become Eve. Adam was the bearer of unconscious amorous incompetence. He becomes aware of this incompetence through the externalization of Eve. He acquires a conscious amorous skill by uniting with her. It is by fully inte-

---

89 *Le Seigneur et le Satan* by Annick de Souzenelle, p. 133-139 (Paris: Albin Michel, 2016). On this subject, we should also turn to the remarkable text *Les Arcanes* by Oskar Władysław de Lubicz Miłosz (La Bégude de Mazenc, Fr: Arma Artis, reissued 2016).

grating her that this skill can become unconscious again, fully participating in her completed nature. It is Love that liberates, it is Love that attracts the *Shekinah*, the feminine part of divinity that opens the door of the Heart. Any sanctuary is sacred only by the presence of the *Shekinah*, which according to A.D. Grad,[90] manifests itself between the square and the compass.[91]

The Tetragrammaton clearly indicates the passage from the ternary to the quaternary by the doubling of a Letter. The IHVH, Iod, He, Vav, He has a doubling of He, just as INRI has a doubling of I. In Hebrew, the four letters I, N, R, I evoke the water or the sea *(Iam)*, the fire *(Nur)*, the breath *(Ruach)*, the salt of the earth *(Iabeshah)*. In alchemy, the ternary *Sulfur—Salt—Mercury* calls for another Mercury.

The ternary IVH—*Iod*, the Father, *Vav*, the Son, and *He*, the Holy Spirit—becomes quaternary by doubling the *He*. Leon Bloy had insisted in his time on the intimate connection between the Holy Spirit, Lucifer as bearer of the Light, the Paraclete, and the Woman. *He* is doubled to generate the feminine principle that will unite with *Iod* as masculine principle. The *He* constitutes the creative energy that is designated by the Celestial Virgin, the Mother of the world, Mary or even ISIS whose letters indicate the serpentine power implementing the creative potentiality of *Iod*. This is why Louis Cattiaux[92] tells us: "The holy Name of God is an all-powerful magic in the mouth of him who truly believes and loves."

---

90 *Le meurtre fondamental* by A.D. Grad (Nice, Fr: Alain Lefeuvre, 1981).

91 For A.D. Grad, from the line determined by the two columns Jakin and Boaz, as far as the East, is drawn the closed garden, the *gan noul*, "a characteristically female area sealed between the branches of the square and the compass."

92 *The Message Rediscovered* by Louis Cattiaux, XVII: 23 (Barcelona: Beya, 2005).

These few indications, inscribed clearly or implicitly in the rituals of the Rectified Scottish Rite, establish the possibility, undoubtedly infinitely plural, of the liberation of the dualistic darkness by a conscious reorientation towards the nondual light. If, as Martines de Pasqually suggests, God engendered the Spirit that begot the soul that begot the body, the body can be reintegrated into the soul, the soul into the Spirit, the Spirit into God. This way of Reintegration, way of the Body of Glory, also evokes the *Merkabah.*

It is again Yohanan Ben Zakkai, and other rabbis of antiquity, who develop the pre-Kabbalistic tradition of (the) *Merkabah,* a Hebrew word translated as "chariot." This tradition is based on the first chapter of Ezekiel in the *Mishnah Hagigah.* To cross the darkness of the insurmountable abyss between the soul and the divine Throne, a chariot is needed, a vehicle of Light, a body of Glory, the *Merkabah.* Now, if the hexagram that structures the symbol of the degree of Scottish Master of Saint Andrew, like the Martinist pentacle drawn by Saint-Martin, is projected from a two-dimensional world into a three-dimensional world, we find ourselves in the presence of the symbol of the vehicle of the *Merkabah.*[93] Operative Companions, especially carpenters,[94] teach that to build the *Merkabah,* it is first of all necessary to master the Platonic solids: the cube, symbol of the Earth; the icosahedron and its twenty sides, symbol of water; the octahedron, symbol of the air; the tetrahedron and its four sides, symbol of fire; and the dodecahedron, twelve faces, symbol of the ether, the Universe, the Whole.[95]

---

93 Additionally, the *Merkabah* is inscribed in a cube. For some operative Companions, the *Cubic Stone* of the Freemasons would be a misinterpretation of the *Merkabah* planted in the ground to ensure its stability.

94 The carpenter Companion realizes the drawing from the sphere, then the calculation; from the sphere, he makes an assembly of six crosses. The stonemason Companion draws from the sphere and generates a cube for machining. The roofing or locksmith Companion realizes the drawing from the sphere he then develops and by folding the six points, he assembles and welds.

95 The tradition of Kepler's polygons associates the tetrahedron with Mars, the cube with Jupiter, the octahedron with Mercury, the dodecahedron with the earth and the icosahedron with Saturn. In the Kabbalah, the *Merkabah* may be associated with the Sephirah *Daath,* the tetrahedron with *Binah,* the cube with *Geburah,* the octahedron with *Hod,* the dodecahedron with *Yesod* and the icosahedron with *Malkut.*

Platonic solids (convex regular polyhedra)

| *Tetrahedron* | *Hexahedron or Cube* | *Octahedron* | *Dodecahedron* | *Icosahedron* |

To conclude and to make sense within the setting of the Rectified Scottish Rite, our operative Companions also teach us that the dualistic geometry of the line is powerless to assemble certain Platonic solids to make a full volume. It is necessary to apply a "rectification" of four tenths of the unit[96] (4–10–1), which is, symbolically, the tetrad, the decad, and the One. And to assert the adage: "The Orient is worth the line."

---

96 2 × 2 or two tenths for each of the two faces concerned, one for each adjacent volume.

10   Martinism and Gnostic Churches

THE RELATIONSHIP BETWEEN MARTINISM and the Church in general, Gnostic Church(es) in particular, was and remains singularly complex, a source of many disillusions, wanderings, and excesses, sometimes just useless and at other times toxic. Their relations, from certain angles, are also sometimes fruitful. We are not in these few pages going to set forth the whole history of the Gnostic Church and its relation to the Martinist current—we shall leave this to the historians who are interested in the question. We simply wish to recall what is essential in order to know, as Robert Amadou expressed, under the name of T. Jacques in the brochure *Qu'est-ce que l'Église Gnostique?*[97] that "Every particular church, and the universal Church, are Gnostic by definition and strive to become so by construction."

It is interesting to remember the project of Jules-Benoit Stanislas Doinel du Val-Michel (1842-1903), the founder of the instituted Gnostic Church. This Freemason from the Grand Orient of France was also a practicing spiritualist at a time when the spiritualist movement was not without interest. It is in the movement of French spiritualist circles that the Gnostic Church was born.

---

97 *Qu'est-ce que l'Église Gnostique?* by T. Jacques (Guérigny, Fr: CIREM, 1996).

Following several visions or communications, Jules Doinel wanted to restore the celebration of the feminine aspect of God. In 1888, Jules Doinel felt consecrated by the "æon Jesus" to build a new Church in this direction.

Close to Lady Caithness, an eminent figure in spiritualist circles, Jules Doinel one day received the following message during a seance:

> *I address you because you are my friend, my servant, and the prelate of my Albigensian Church. I am exiled from the Pleroma, and I am the one Valentin named Sophia-Achamoth. I am the one Simon the Magician called Helen-Ennoia; for I am the Eternal Androgyne. Jesus is the Word of God; I am the Thought of God. One day, I will go back to my Father, but I need help to do this; the supplication of my Brother Jesus is required to intercede for me. Only the Infinite can save the Infinite, and only God is able to save God. Listen carefully: The One first produced the One, and then One. And the Three are only One: the Father, the Word, and the Thought. Establish my Gnostic Church. The Demiurge will be powerless against her. Receive the Paraclete.*

Other messages followed. Whatever the nature of these experiments, anomalous or pathological, they were at the origin of a movement whose influence remains. Doinel proclaimed in 1890 the beginning of the "Era of Restored Gnosis." He founded the Gnostic Church under the mystical name of Valentin II, as a tribute to the founder of the Gnostic School of the fifth century. From this spiritual and timeless ordination were to flow multiple temporal lineages of Gnostic bishops and small churches.

Among the first bishops consecrated by Jules Doinel, we find several personalities of the Martinist current and of the occultist scene of the Belle Époque: Papus of course, Gérard d'Encausse (1865-1916), Tau Vincent—Sedir, Yvon Le Loup (1871-1926), Tau

Paul—Chamuel, Lucien Mauchel (1867-1936), Tau Bardesane—Louis-Sophrone Fugairon, Tau Sophronius—Fabre des Essarts (1848-1917), Tau Synesius, etc.

In 1890, Papus invited Jules Doinel into the Supreme Council of the Martinist Order. The ties of intimacy between the Martinist Order of Papus and the Gnostic Church of Doinel are therefore initiated from the beginning of the adventure without the Gnostic Church ever being the "official" church of the Martinist Order. If some have wished for it and still wish it, there is a real danger there that goes beyond the Martinist Order and the Gnostic Church themselves, since the Rectified Scottish Rite is also experiencing difficulties when certain dignitaries want to impose a religious formalism no matter what it is. The Church of the Martinists is indeed the interior church, according to Louis-Claude de Saint-Martin,[98] through its multiple formal expressions (which we must often guard against), as well as its non-formal expressions, and above all through its permanence. "Unity is hardly found in associations; it is found only in our individual junction with God. It is only after it is done that we naturally find ourselves brothers to each other," insists Louis-Claude de Saint-Martin.[99]

The ambiguity remains as to the place of the Gnostic Church (or one of its multiple avatars) in relation to the Martinist Order. It regularly causes disturbances, schisms, and adjustments. In 1911, a treaty governing its relations was adopted. It was renewed and clarified in 1968. The primary function of the Gnostic

---

98 To examine this central question more deeply, read the works of Jean-Marc Vivenza: *L'Église et le sacerdoce selon Louis-Claude de Saint-Martin* (Hyères, Fr: La Pierre Philosophale, 2013); *Le culte « en esprit » de l'Église intérieure* (Hyères, Fr: La Pierre Philosophale, 2014), and *Le mystère de l'Église intérieure ou la « naissance » de Dieu dans l'âme* (Hyères, Fr: La Pierre Philosophale, 2016).

99 *Mon portrait historique et philosophique (1789-1803)*, published by Robert Amadou (Paris: Julliard, 1961).

Church and its descendants is to allow, in the discretion required for any truly initiatory work, Martinists, but also Freemasons, Pythagoreans, Rosicrucians, or others, to participate in the Christian mysteries in all their sacramental dimension without seeing themselves trapped in an organizational apparatus that is binding or even hostile to their quest.

Since Jules Doinel and his spiritualist ordination, the Gnostic churches have not ceased seeking to "normalize" themselves from the apostolic point of view by inscribing themselves in the classical episcopal filiations. Thus, since 1913, the Gnostic churches have taken their apostolic succession from the Syrian Church of Antioch.

We reproduce below the last version of the two genealogical tables compiled by Robert Amadou.[100]

The original project of Jules Doinel, laudable as it was, to consider Gnosis as the true religion and to celebrate the feminine mystery of God, was somewhat abused over time, first by Doinel himself who, in 1895, abdicated his charge and, following an enantiodromic process (the tendency of things to change into their very opposite, already described by Plutarch) well known in the esoteric world, attacked his creation under the pseudonym of Jean Kostka[101] and collaborated with Leo Taxil, only to ask, five years later, for his reinstatement within the Gnostic Church, which had endured.

Gnostic churches have often Romanized, and many occultist or hermetic members of the Gnostic priestly body transform themselves into Bible-thumpers at the approach of death, far from any awakening metaphysics. Instead of shedding their conditioning, they shut themselves up in the dualistic tensions of ec-

---

100 *Qu'est-ce que l'Église Gnostique?* by T. Jacques (Guérigny, Fr: CIREM, 1996). Appendix Tables.

101 *Lucifer démasqué* by Jean Kotska (Paris: Dualpha, 2009).

clesiastical forms.

Few remember Doinel's intention with regard to the sacred feminine and few have sought to implement what the very Catholic Leon Bloy (1846-1917) knew perfectly: the identity between the Woman, Lucifer (the Bearer of Light), the Paraclete, and the Holy Spirit. Armand Toussaint (1895-1994), a portrait of whom you will find in the appendix this book, was one of the few to deploy the feminine dimension of God in his Rosicrucian Apostolic Church and to maintain the discipline of the mystery.

Today, the traditional current of Gnostic churches continues, avoiding the disturbance caused by too much visibility and despite the proliferation of counterfeits at the beginning of the millennium.

THE APOSTOLIC SUCCESSION
IN THE GNOSTIC CHURCH

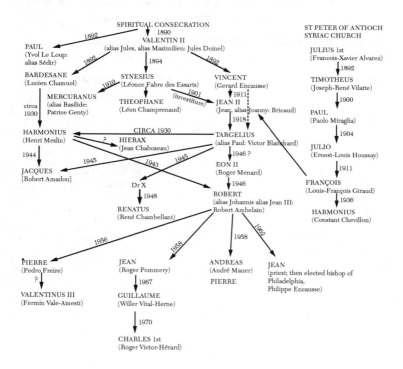

SPIRITUAL CONSECRATION
1890
VALENTIN II
(alias Jules, alias Maximilien: Jules Doinel)

PAUL
(Yvol Le Loup:
alias Sédir)

BARDESANE
(Lucien Chamuel)

MERCURANUS
(alias Basilide:
Patrice Genty)
circa
1930

HARMONIUS
(Henri Meslin)

1944

JACQUES
[Robert Amadou]

SYNESIUS
(Léonce Fabre des Essarts)

THEOPHANE
(Léon Champrenaud)

CIRCA 1930
HIERAX
(Jean Chaboseau)

Dr X
1948

RENATUS
(René Chambellant)

VINCENT
(Gerard Encausse)

1911
JEAN II
(Jean, alias Joanny: Bricaud)
1918

TARGELIUS
(alias Paul: Victor Blanchard)

1946 ?

EON II
(Roger Menard)

1946

ROBERT
(alias Johannis alias Jean III:
Robert Ambelain)

ST PETER OF ANTIOCH
SYRIAC CHURCH

JULIUS 1st
(Francois-Xavier Alvarez)
1892

TIMOTHEUS
(Joseph-René Vilatte)
1900

PAUL
(Paolo Miraglia)
1904

JULIO
(Ernest-Louis Houssay)
1911

FRANÇOIS
(Louis-François Giraud)
1936

HARMONIUS
(Constant Chevillon)

PIERRE
(Pedro Freire)
?

VALENTINUS III
(Fermin Vale-Amesti)

JEAN
(Roger Pommery)
1967

GUILLAUME
(Willer Vital-Herne)

1970

CHARLES 1st
(Roger Victor-Hérard)

ANDREAS
(André Mauer)
PIERRE

JEAN
(priest; then elected bishop of
Philadelphia,
Philippe Encausse)

1892 · 1894 · 1892 · 1910 · 1901 (investiture) · 1930 · 1945 · 1943 · 1945 · 1956 · 1958 · 1958 · 1962

GNOSTIC CHURCHES AND PATRIARCHS

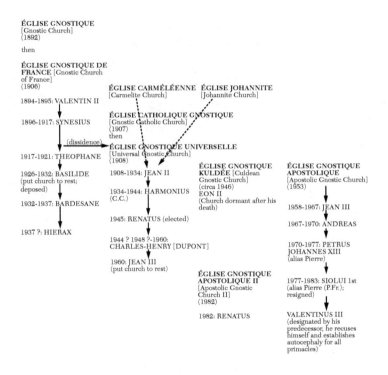

ÉGLISE GNOSTIQUE
[Gnostic Church]
(1892)

then

ÉGLISE GNOSTIQUE DE
FRANCE [Gnostic Church
of France]
(1906)

ÉGLISE CARMÉLÉENNE   ÉGLISE JOHANNITE
[Carmelite Church]   [Johannite Church]

1894-1895: VALENTIN II

ÉGLISE CATHOLIQUE GNOSTIQUE
[Gnostic Catholic Church]
(1907)
then

1896-1917: SYNESIUS

(dissidence)

1917-1921: THEOPHANE

ÉGLISE GNOSTIQUE UNIVERSELLE
[Universal Gnostic Church]
(1908)

1908-1934: JEAN II

ÉGLISE GNOSTIQUE
KULDÉE [Culdean
Gnostic Church]
(circa 1946)
EON II
(Church dormant after his
death)

ÉGLISE GNOSTIQUE
APOSTOLIQUE
[Apostolic Gnostic Church]
(1953)

1926-1932: BASILIDE
(put church to rest;
deposed)

1934-1944: HARMONIUS
(C.C.)

1932-1937: BARDESANE

1945: RENATUS (elected)

1958-1967: JEAN III

1937 ?: HIERAX

1944 ? 1948 ?-1960:
CHARLES-HENRY [DUPONT]

1967-1970: ANDREAS

1960: JEAN III
(put church to rest)

1970-1977: PETRUS
JOHANNES XIII
(alias Pierre)

ÉGLISE GNOSTIQUE
APOSTOLIQUE II
[Apostolic Gnostic
Church II]
(1982)

1977-1983: SIOLUI 1st
(alias Pierre (P.Fr.);
resigned)

1982: RENATUS

VALENTINUS III
(designated by his
predecessor, he recuses
himself and establishes
autocephaly for all
primacies)

11   Charter for XXIst Century Gnostic Churches

In tribute to T. Jacques (Robert Amadou)[102]

Introduction

Throughout the past century, the history of the Gnostic churches has remained rich and eventful. On the fringes of the Martinist Order founded by Papus and his like, the Gnostic Church spread out into many branches. This tree was the fruit of the very principle of the Gnostic movement composed of free communities.

The Gnostic Churches and Circles throughout the last century were crucibles that allowed the illuminist, occultist, and hermetic currents to continue and flourish. The freedom, the tolerance, and the spirit of inquiry that dominated this constantly

---

102 Robert Amadou greatly contributed to the reflection on the missions of the Gnostic churches, particularly with the text *Qu'est-ce que l'Église gnostique?*, created in collaboration with T. Antoine and published in 1996 by the International Center for Martinist Research and Studies (CIREM). That document served as the basis for the drafting of this Charter, built on the same principle as the *Charter for XXIst Century Martinist Orders,* proposed by CIREM on the occasion of the bicentennial of the death of Louis-Claude de Saint-Martin. We especially thank Denis Labouré for his essential contribution to the finalization of this charter.

renewed movement allowed many questers to find themselves, independently of their particular paths, in true companionship, despite some inevitable vicissitudes.

The Gnostic movement of the churches was also able to welcome other currents into its midst to preserve them and help them to experience new development.

Today, so that this state of mind remains and that what is alive does not become fixed, the simple principles that have contributed to their influence are inscribed in this *Charter for XXIst Century Gnostic Churches*.

The adoption of this Charter is free. It confers no rights, only the duties that derive from ethics. No one will have to give an account of it except to himself and to Providence.

Source: CIREM. Copying encouraged.

1. A Gnostic is one who has received the Holy Spirit, this feminine wind, both breath and fire.

2. A Christian, therefore "living," is one who bathes in the fire of the Spirit, and in whom this fire works. Letting himself be worked by it, he moves towards the total man, the completed man, that is to say, *the* Man.

3. *Gnosis* or *Knowledge* predates the appearance of Christianity. It can be defined as "the knowledge of God in me and of me, in God," or "of transcendence in immanence and immanence in transcendence."

4. *Gnosis* is by nature neither dualistic nor non-dualistic, even if the temporal gnostic expressions are necessarily marked by a functional dualism.

5. The Church has a community aspect and an individual aspect. She is the community of men and women working towards their deification. She is simultaneously an inner reality and an experience of the deifying action of each being by the Holy Spirit.

6. The real Church pre-exists in Christ before any institutional expression. Whether they are "big" churches or more low-profile organizations, these visible manifestations are churches of desire, not human places that hold an exclusive truth.

7. The ministries, ordained in the Holy Spirit, transmitted in apostolic succession, legitimized by the community, assured by the continuity of the works of the Apostles and of the disciples, men and women, represent the sole pastor and priest, the Christ. There is therefore neither a "new church" nor a "church holding secret rites."

8. If the real Church is invisible, she beckons through prayer, the sacraments, baptism, the Eucharist, and the Scriptures.

9. The Church is realized through the celebration of the Eucharist in all its dimensions (symbolic, alchemical, metaphysical, theurgic, sacramental...)

10. The Old Testament and the New Testament are intimately connected in a meaningful unity. The Bible, supplemented by apocryphal Gospels, should be read as opening a way to Christ.

11. Beyond languages and through languages, the Scriptures are offered in four senses, literal (or historical), allegorical (or typological), tropological (or ethical), and anagogical (or mystical), the last of which is transcendent and infinite.

12. Dogmas are understood, just as for the first Christians, not as truths, expressed, but as privileged vehicles of the mysteries.

13. Mary is *"forma dei"* (the active mold of God). By meditating on the mystery of Mary, the Gnostic reaches the state of the molten metal and throws himself into it. Thus takes place the gestation of his new life, which announces deification by grace.

14. In Christ, a complete man, pure and simple, every Christian is united with all beings and all forms of life which he recognizes as not separate from himself.

15. The constituted Gnostic Churches are an ephemeral expression, both distant echo and celebration, of the real Church or Mystical Body of Christ.

16. The Christian is reintegrated, and more, while his body of glory is built up by liturgy, and aided by theurgy and alchemy, according to astrological protocol. Every day of this life, his inner man is renewed: sown psychically, he is transfigured spiritually, while his soul is embodied. From now on he receives the deposit for the future life. It transmutes likewise the matter of the world.[103]

17. Christ dwells in this world by the blood and water that gushed out of his side. Hidden from the world in the very world they transfigure, the chalice that gathers them appears to pure hearts.

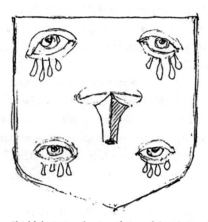

Shield depicting the Crucifixion of the Christ
Stained Glass of the Chapter Hall in Batalha (Portugal) 1514
Drawing by Lima de Freitas

---

103 According to a passage from the book *De la Sainte Science* by Robert Amadou.

12   Gnosis

"Make way for the Spirit"
Louis-Claude de Saint-Martin

MARTINISM IS PART OF THE CURRENT of Illuminism. It is the flag-
ship. Martinism is mystical and mysterious, which determines its
gnostic specificity.[104] It is not a religious gnosis, which connects,
but a gnosis that loosens and liberates. Gnosis[105] dispenses with
the religion and the church that alienate the man of the stream by
instilling, consciously or unconsciously, the dualistic presupposi-
tion that fuels the process of the identification of consciousness.
Moreover, Gnosis, being a radiation without form, ignores religion, the vital impetus of form.

We have often said that initiation begins with a counter-
spirituality. This assertion is often badly received and deserves
further explanation. Man in religion falls back into a spirituality
of the "person," a concept of spirituality that can convey the presence of the Absolute, but which encloses it at the same time in a

---

104 From *Introduction à la littérature gnostique I, collections retrouvées
avant 1945* by Michel Tardieu and Jean-Daniel Dubois (Paris: Cerf and
CNRS, 1986). Michel Tardieu in a *Historique du mot « gnostique »* identifies eight different uses of the word among authors, ancient, modern,
or contemporary: epistemological, obvious, heresiological, clementine,
evagrian, esoteric, syncretistic and psychological. We will use here the
epistemological sense of "pure knowledge."

105 From ecclesiastical Greek: *gnosis,* "knowledge."

web of representations that can proceed all the way to uncompromising dogma. That these representations, these conceptions, are momentarily attuned, beautiful, creative, and even nourished by experience is of little importance. They crystallize and become limits, boundaries, walls, as soon as there is identification and as soon as their transitory and medial character is forgotten. The imaginary freezes the imaginal. The initiatory process truly unfolds in Silence, outside of concept, outside of spirituality, and outside of religion. True Spirituality, that of Being, dissolves conceptual spiritualities.

This true Spirituality is Gnosis, perfect knowledge that can not be circumscribed by any model or any doctrine. This "being born with" annihilates the distinction between subject and object in the One-Being. Gnosis is accomplished outside of dialectic and outside of dialogue, but can shed light on the latter, when the dialogue is informed both by the experience of Gnosis and its permanence. Gnosis, perfect or absolute knowledge, should not be confused with the causal knowledge that veils the Self or the Real. Causal knowledge resides in the movement of cause-effect, which weaves the forgetting body of our true nature. This causal knowledge, or ignorance, is at the origin of the coagulation of the ego, characterized by duality.[106] Awareness of ignorance, of the illusory play of causality, frees one from the grip of the ego. Rig-

---

106 "Gnosis, or Knowledge, therefore necessarily excludes all dualism and duality. It is beyond oppositions, for metaphysical reasons. One, invariable, and eternal, it is reflected in every tradition of which it constitutes the generative and governing modality, as it nourishes its esotericism. Centered and manifested totality, essence, and substance as a principal reality, gnosis is 'unique' and, as such, can be considered as the 'milieu' from which all proceed, through which all subsist, and in which all end. The supreme degree of salvific reality and metaphysical expression, it is thus the 'Center of all Centers,' as a litany of the Heart of Jesus says, and as such is the symbolic location of the Word in this divine anthropomorphosis of Christ. (...)

orous practice, as we have seen, is necessary for this purpose. Absolute knowledge dissolves causal knowledge. Gnosis then floods consciousness.

Martinism conveys two conceptions of transmission that are not mutually exclusive, but on the contrary are associated in the reality of the initiatory experience. The Martinism "of Louis-Claude de Saint-Martin" offers a direct way, immediate access to perfect knowledge, to Gnosis, with no other intermediary than Silence which then makes the initiate another Christ, a New Man. This Gnosis inscribed in the Self, but not circumscribed to the Self, can violate a psychic apparatus unprepared for this ultimate experience which is a death to the world and a death of the conceived world. Traditions help the reception, assimilation, and wise cataloging of this experience, which is essential rather than existential, precisely in existence.[107]

Very classically, and like the great traditional currents, Martinism, more broadly Illuminism, considers Gnosis as knowledge that can be transmitted over time, both by teaching and by practice. The teaching is organized around principles resulting from a revelation considered of divine origin and of which we will not forget that if it originates in the experience of Being, it is colored according to the language and the culture which claim to convey

---

"Consequently, in the Christian symbolism of the Cross, the non-figuration of the human body is not a negation of the latter—perfectly authentic at its level of reality, and moreover exemplary representative of this level. What is denied is the psychosomatic 'ego' considered as a model or divine stasis." Jean Tourniac in *De la Chevalerie au secret du Temple* (Paris: Dervy, 2008).

107 On this point, we will join Jean Borella who in an article entitled *Gnose et gnosticisme chez René Guénon* affirms: "Gnosis is at the same time ineffable and interior, a spiritual state, and also formulatable and objective, a doctrinal corpus. From this point of view, it is transmissible and can be the object of a tradition." In *Dossier H René Guénon* (Paris: L'Age d'Homme, 1984).

it. If Tradition is of divine origin, it is not found, as such, outside this point of origin. There is thus a progressive, gradualist,
temporal, and tempered transmission, which passes through the
mysteries, the rites, the arts, and the symbols that Jacob Bœhme
tells us are "the signature of things." Tradition irrigates, more
or less, specific traditions. Gnosis manifests itself, more or less
equally, in particular gnosticisms.

We are in the presence of two modes of assimilation of Gnosis.
One operates from the center to the periphery, the direct way,
the other from the periphery to the center, the progressive way.
It is, in the end, the same circle and the same center based on an
experience that is "imperience."

Illuminism refers to light and gnosticism to knowledge. There
is no light without knowledge nor knowledge without light.
These are the two legs of the New Man who can thus recover, in
a movement of elevation that is reintegration according to the
Réau-Croix, realization according to the Rose-Croix, and rectification according to the Beneficent Knights of the Holy City, after having "killed" death. This death and resurrection constitute
the symbolic and operative heart of the initiatory process, which
is based on a Wisdom and a High Science of transmutation. Alchemy, the chemistry of "the One of whom nothing can be said"
is everywhere present, at each stage, at each access, of this path
towards individuation which leads to the realization of the Great
Work.

In Martinism, in the most encompassing sense of the term,
this death of death that gives divine life requires the action of the
"good companion spirit," or "holy guardian angel," an aspect of
our ultimate reality, from our future deification, the simultaneity of alpha and omega. If faith can take man out of the stream,
it can not help him to verticalize the desire, to decondition it.
Asceticism dissolves faith, which remains a personal impetus. It

establishes transparency and edifies the individual. The luminous attraction of Being, highlighted by the "good companion spirit," replaces faith.

Gnosis is said to be universal. It is, when there is no more universe. Universality, in the world of forms, is an illusion. There is no expressed truth that can claim universality without immediately constituting a division, without slicing this so-called universality in two. If there is universality, it is hidden in the intimate, in the very intimate, where words cease to have meaning and silence teaches, where being is in communion, where the experience-imperience is nondual.

It is not a question of rejecting gnosticisms under the pretext of Gnosis, but of measuring their relations, of following their derivatives to better prevent the (always possible) drift, and of entering into an intimate form of mathematics and geometry, to which analogies and correspondences do indeed lead.

Gnosis, which says the inexpressible, the nature of the Real, Gnosis, absent from representations, rejects nothing, inhabits all things and all reproduction. Things act as access to *"la Chose,"*[108] almost in spite of themselves. Robert Amadou noted the proximity in the Castilian language of the two words *cosa* and *causa*. Where *la Chose* manifests itself, the "cause" is heard and this cause is none other than Gnosis.

The quest is not speculative, it is operative. That is to say: in love. That is to say: wise. Love of the divine, of the Absolute. Wisdom of the divine, of the Absolute. Gnosis makes of the one who receives it, or who is received within it, an unknown theosopher, necessarily unknown.

Let's leave the conclusion to Robert Amadou:

---

108 "The Thing." Object of the primitive worship of the Elus Coëns and object of reintegration according to Martines de Pasqually, *la Chose* is omnipresent and indefinable.

For, if Christ is God and the new man is another Christ, the Christian theurgist needs, in order to return and contribute to the return of every being emanated from the Principle, only to regenerate himself. To this end he must possess Wisdom, and start by looking for it.

This search, this possession is called 'theosophy.' And its instrument is called 'will.'[109]

---

109 *La magie des Élus Coëns. Théurgie. Instruction secrète.* Fonds Z. *Les manuscrits réservés du Philosophe inconnu.* Published by Robert Amadou (Paris: Cariscript, 1988).

13   Grace

ROBERT AMADOU LIKED TO REPEAT that nothing was possible without Grace and that even a personality like Gurdjieff insisted on this necessity, the necessity of Grace. But what are we talking about exactly? Certainly not that diffuse and common feeling, which prevails too often, of a somewhat magical or miraculous and random intervention. The question of Grace is as fundamental and inseparable from the Time of Lilies as it is from the Time of Roses that comes after, or better, through the Time of Thorns.

The Cistercian monk Joachim de Fiore announced the three ages we will find in the *Trovas* of the prophet Bandarra:

- The era of the Old Testament, age of the Father, which begins with Abraham and ends with the birth of Christ. The Time of Thorns.
- The era of the New Testament, age of the Son, the Time of Grace or Roses, which begins with the last king of Israel, Hosea (732-724 BC) and develops with St. John the Baptist and Jesus.
- The era of the coming World, age of the Holy Spirit,[110] or the Time of Lilies, underlying the other two, but explicit with the return of the Prophet Elijah to continue until the Last Judgment. This is the time of the permanent miracle of Grace.

---

110   Joachim de Fiore had fixed this descent of the Holy Spirit in 1260.

These three ages become five times according to António Vieira[111] who, after the death of King Sebastian in 1578, revisited and revived, in the perspective of a Fifth Empire, the prophecies of Bandarra (1500-1556) from the dream of Nebuchadnezzar reported in the prophecy of Daniel.[112] Father Vieira announced the advent of the Fifth and last Empire of a thousand years succeeding the Assyrian, Persian, Greek, and Roman (extending into the Holy Roman) empires. The Assyrian Empire is that of the Father, the Persian Empire is that of the Father and the Son, the Greek Empire that of the Son, and the Roman Empire that of the Son and the Holy Spirit. The Portuguese or Lusitanian Empire marks the reign of the Spirit, represented by Sebastian who assumes the function of the priest-king of Christ, similar to that of the mythical Prester John, whom certain missions in the Age of Discoveries sought in Africa and then in India. Vieira places this Empire under a double authority, that of the King of Portugal and that of the Pope.[113]

Fernando Pessoa specified the nature of this union thus:

Thus, we are certain that in the Fifth Empire there will be the reunion of forces that have been separated for a long time, but which have been coming together for a long time: the left side

111   The Jesuit António Vieira (1608-1697), a major figure of Portugal, considered the "father of the Portuguese language."

112   The *Trovas* were collected in 1540. We are therefore long before the birth of Sebastian. They won Bandarra a condemnation by the Holy Office. Later, António Vieira interpreted the *Trovas* in a hermeneutic modality. What are prophecies at this time? They are not mere intuitions or the fruit of a work of divination, of some kind of augury. They are part of a vision in the Imaginal, of an access to the divine ideas which need to be precipitated in temporality not as a possibility, but as a truth.

113   For a deeper understanding of this theme, read *Correspondance imaginale. Lima de Freitas & Gilbert Durand.* Preface by Michel Cazenave. Edited by Rémi Boyer (Bégude de Mazenc, Fr: Arma Artis, 2016).

of knowledge—science, reasoning, intellectual speculation; and
its right side—occult knowledge, intuition, mystical and cabalistic
speculation. The alliance of Sebastian, Emperor of the World, and
the Angelic Pope represents this intimate alliance, this fusion of
the material and the spiritual, perhaps without separation.[114]

The time of the Fifth Empire, Empire of the Holy or Free Spirit,
is no longer a matter of *Chronos*, but of *Aion*, and even more of
Kairos. It is the Time of the Outpouring of Grace. *Chronos, Aion,*
and *Kairos,* just like the distinctions between the times—the
Times of Thorns, Roses, Lilies or others—must be understood as
states of consciousness, states of Consciousness, really in total
simultaneity, but potentially actualizable in a differentiated way
within duality.

Grace is of course central to the operativity of the sacraments.
It is more broadly the essential dimension of any initiation that
is diffusive of Grace. It is first of all *virtus,* grace as the spiritual
energy of the sacrament, then, since the deepening of the twelfth
century, *res,* grace as the profoundest reality of the sacrament,
la Chose or the *cause* of the Order of Knight Masons Elus Coëns
of the Universe.

We readily speak of the "gift of grace." There is an intimate
dimension of Grace, this free and active love of the Absolute, particularly present in the death and resurrection of Christ and in
the action of the Holy Spirit, a non-historical event in reality that
we live through moment to moment. The Absolute forgets itself
in duality and gives itself in an infinite number of ways, always
new, in order to recognize itself through each form of life. There
is a dialogue, a conversation of God with Himself that aims at

---

114   Fernando Pessoa, *Obra Poética e em Prosa,* Tome III, introduction, organization, bibliography and notes by Antonio Quadros (Porto,
Pt: Lello et Frères, 1986).

conversion, the recognition of oneself as God through the many. This intimate dialogue, this co-creativity, arouses and awakens our intrinsic freedom, the very freedom of God.

Initiation carries, or should carry, by the action of Fire, a sacramental power, that of Grace. In the Illuminist stream in general, Martinism in particular, we can suggest that the cardiac way, the "formation of the heart," makes it possible to "acquire" or "receive" Grace, the two verbs being inappropriate. At every moment, in the crypt of the heart, from inhalation to exhalation and exhalation to inhalation, on the river of breath, by the passage of the death and resurrection of Christ and the reception of his spirit, we enter into eternal life. It is the advent of the New Man of Louis-Claude de Saint-Martin and the full entry into the New Covenant, announced by the prophets, the aggregation to the living body of Christ. The transformation is not spectacular, it is deep, intimate, nuptial, and never mundane.

Grace is a pneumatological anointing, redemptive, reintegrative, and inclusive of all that is manifested. If God begets the Spirit that begets the soul that begets the body, the body is reintegrated into the soul, reintegrated into the Spirit, and reintegrated into God. It is the movement of Grace perceived as the self-communication of God with Himself, self-communication that leads to a self-communion, a movement that goes from duality to nonduality, from the multiple to the One. Everything is consciously transformed into Love.

Leonardo Coimbra (1883-1936) in a wonderful work, *A Alegria, a Dor e a Graça*,[115] magnificently painted this movement of reintegration. First we have dualistic love, a source of joy, then the pain of separation that awakens to nonduality and finally the Grace of non-separation through nondualistic love. Leonardo Coimbra

---

115 *A Alegria, a Dor e a Graça* by Leonardo Coimbra (Porto, Pt: Renascença portuguesa, 1916).

also tells us in one of his magnificent intuitions: "Freedom exists and grace is its body." Grace as the body of Freedom, of the absolute Freedom of God, of the Lord or of the Self, is also its conscious realization.

Let us conclude again with Leonardo Coimbra:

> Solitude and Silence give us a sense of immediate presence and integral fullness; it is not God felt in the inner repetition of a movement that encompasses All, it is the Divine Grace poured out throughout the Being, like certain maternal kisses, floating on the infantile face in liquid smiles of happiness.
>
> Like the traveler who, when he arrives at the summit, rests his sight on the freshness of the streams and loses his eyes in the sky, yet will never forget the earth, so thought, arrived at Grace, is an immediate prayer, a hymn of praise and joy, in which all imperfections reduce the laborious and dramatic body to an eternal meaning of communication and love.
>
> It is the Invisible, the Ineffable, the Unnamed who populates all Solitude, who fills the whole of Silence with cosmic and substantial words.[116]

Let's enter the Order of the Time of Lilies...

---

116   Ibid., p. 194.

Appendices

Appendix 1

Spiritual Exercises for Bears and Knights[117]

Bear & Knight

It may seem surprising to associate in a title the bear and the knight as companions. Imagination is not lacking in initiatory battles between a warrior and a bear after which the man or, more rarely, the woman, conqueror of the king of animals, becomes a knight.

Formerly, many traditions, in particular Celtic, Slavic, German, and others, made of the bear an equal of the human being. These traditions lasted until the twelfth century, a time when the Church, hostile to the permanence of these pagan roots, succeeded in eradicating all bear worship.

The name Arthur, founding king of the Round Table, synthesizes in itself the secret and sacred bond that unites the bear and the human. The bear is the king of animals. It therefore typifies royalty and the association of the monarch with the mark of the

---

117 This set of practices was first published in a bilingual Portuguese-French version in the book *Chevalerie, Franc-Maçonnerie et Spiritualité—Exercices Spirituels pour les Ours et les Chevaliers, Cavalaria, Maçonaria e Espiritualidade—Exercicios Espirituais para Ursos e Cavaleiros* by Rémi Boyer and Michel Bédaton. Illustrations by Jean-Michel Nicollet (Guérigny, Fr: CIREM, Sintra, Pt: Zefiro and Arcane Zero, 2015).

bear signifies the royal function. The etymology of the name Arthur evokes the bear-king. The possible sources of the word refer
to strength, power, and the absence of fear, qualities of the warrior who aspires to Chivalry. A totemic animal in some forms of
shamanism, it also adorned many crests of knights. We refer the
reader to the remarkable works of Michel Pastoureau[118] devoted
to the bear to understand in depth the few proposals of this introduction.

The bear goes through the mood swings of nature like the
manifestations of seasonal cycles, even particularly hostile ones,
with astonishing resistance. It lives—just like the knight in his
trials.

Some shamanic ritual forms seek appropriation of the bear's
qualities through trance in order to transform the warrior into an
"invincible bear." Michel Pastoureau speaks of the search for "a
perfect osmosis between the bear and the warrior."

Being an animal psychopomp, the bear also acts through
dreams, warns of danger, saves, initiates, or announces death.

If the bear has a warrior function it also has, like the dragon,
that of mediator between Heaven and Earth, between gods and
human beings. It is both a ferryman and an initiator. A lunar animal, it carries the indirect light of the sun and makes it tolerable
to humans. It is indicated as a sign by a constellation in its name.

It was also a god or goddess in certain Celtic traditions, traces
of which are to be found in various areas of Old Europe, from
Ireland to Bohemia. The hibernation of the bear, whose entry was
celebrated on November 11, corresponds in Arthurian myths to
the occultation of the hero until the expected return on February
2, which corresponds today to Candlemas. The Church, in its desire to kill the symbolic power of the bear, has sought to hide the

---

118   *L'ours. Histoire d'un roi déchu* by Michel Pastoureau (Paris: Le
Seuil, 2007).

bear feasts with major Christian holidays.

If the bear is the equal of man, it is also because of its sexuality. For centuries, it was considered that bears do not mate like quadrupeds, but like humans, which scientific research has denied in modern times. But this belief, like that of the bear's attraction to women's sexual scents, nourished the myth of the union between bear and woman, a union supposed to give birth to heroes, kings, or demigods. These supposed unions were strongly opposed by the Church, but some theologians go so far as to recognize the inter-fertility of woman and bear. This left traces in chivalric and especially Arthurian legends with Yder and even, indirectly, with Tristan. Some large families up to the thirteenth century claimed the symbolic parentage of the bear.

Let us now turn to the following practices related to this kinship of the bear and the human being, especially in its warlike or chivalric function. The bear and the knight on the quest share solitude, wandering, the power to exist, fearlessness, constancy, and the ability to hide, to disappear when darkness reigns and return with the light.

Both must be particularly vigilant in the face of what arises. They must perceive the world as it is to appreciate both its dangers and opportunities. They both carry their own royalty, born of their intrinsic nature that they seek through encounters, like mirrors casting fragmentary reflections of this original and ultimate nature.

In the West, as in the East, certain spiritual practices with a psycho-physical basis, which can be found both among the Jesuits and in Zen Buddhism, are sometimes called the "Way of the Bear." They make it possible to extract oneself from the opaque fabric of conditioning, from identification with the "person," with the "automaton" of Spinoza, which is reminiscent of the "postponed corpse" of Fernando Pessoa, to reconquer the citadel of being through three modes of knowledge—the substance or form, the energy, and finally the essence—which are also three modalities of the work.

The Quadrant of Awakening[119]

The Four Fundamental Techniques

In the decade that preceded the year 2000, that is to say in the 1990s, numerous leaders of traditional movements and organizations as well as some specialists in avant-garde literary, artistic, and philosophical currents, gathered together to exchange and share. A similar experiment had taken place in Italy in the 1930s, not without success.

These very valuable tasks led each participant to examine a shared failure that they had observed. Most members of initiatory organizations seldom addressed the Quest itself, instead getting lost in the many human considerations. Those who succeeded seemed to have been condemned to success, in any case, regardless of the traditional context in which life, God, and the gods had led them to operate.

A workshop was dedicated to establishing a group of techniques that would place the seeker in the exact attitude of the Seeker. Numerous trials were pursued with representative samples of people belonging to various movements, as well as with people not affiliated with any movement in particular. From these experiments, the Quadrant of Awakening was born: a set of four techniques, each of them indispensable and complete (i.e., self-sufficient), and whose particular combination and diligent practice yielded convincing results.

Several leaders of traditional organizations then decided, independently of the current in which they were enrolled, to assign this set of techniques to their members as a required propædeutic. Some avant-garde circles also attempted the experiment.

119 This text has been published several times. It is part of the book *Éveil & incohérisme* by Rémi Boyer (La Bégude de Mazenc, Fr: Arma Artis, 2005).

Note that even more than a propædeutic, many consider the *Quadrant* a way in and of itself, and believe that a discerning mind can find any other way—one that is magical, theurgic, alchemical, and/or awakening—through the *Quadrant.*

In general terms, any Real Way simultaneously consists of a natural magic (according to Giordano Bruno, magic is the art of memory and the manipulation of fantasies; it is the control of what some ethologists call "the bewitchment of the world"), a theurgy, and an alchemy, the vector of a path of immortality.

Our work, in traditional societies, is to lead the possible candidates to Adventure, to perceive the world rather than to ponder it. It is this act of "stopping the world," the successful result of dis-identifying the mind, that allows one to "bend time," for example, a vital skill necessary to embark on the quest. If an individual lives through the experience of breaking with the phenomenal world only once, that person will never—even by completely letting go—confuse the dream and the Real again, even if this rupture with the phenomenal does not necessarily imply an immediate and definitive switch in the reality of Being. It is therefore essential that our practices involve a division of attention.

The four basic practices we propose are a key to achieving this very *attitude,* which allows awakening.

These four practices are the following:

- remembering oneself through the division of attention
- practicing IAO sounds (in both forms)
- the meditation of infinity in the body
- the very important practice of the letter A.

In practicing the four fundamental techniques, the risk we run is to see a process freeze because the "cunning fox" (the mind), sniffing out the trap that would lead it to its own dissolution, will return to its identification and, sometimes very subtly, crystallize what had been released. Our objective, then, is precisely to maintain the rupture, accept the rupture, and to establish a *pleasure* in the rupture.

In summary, we should strive to achieve two goals:

- to make ourselves *capable of asceticism*
- *to awaken the Hermes* within ourselves in order to borrow or to embody the serpentine paths of awakening, so that we can take on the nomadic alternative suitable to the Quest and to the Adventure.

The real paths are made for those who are *real,* who live instead of being lived; they relate to beings rebellious to any form of limitation, unconditional, enamored with freedom, *peaceful and elegant warriors,* elegance being the art of carrying out the smallest gesture that effects the greatest change most favorable to the Quest.

This state of mind stands in opposition to the "bourgeois" state of mind that prevails nowadays, the bourgeois representing Emmanuel Mounier, and ourselves, "the one who is afraid of losing something," whether he is a prince or a vagrant. Yet, along the Real Ways, the adept loses his *self-sufficiency,* that is to say, the intensified pathological need to maintain for others and for himself an image of himself. Without self-image, he could then even lose the identification with the human form. Both of these losses are the price to pay for absolute freedom.

Last but not least, the piece of *evidence* that, as Gurdjieff would say to a certain adept, "Without the grace of God, none of the work would be possible." As soon as this *evidence* is integrated, there is no use dwelling on it. Indeed, as Robert Amadou recalls, "The Real Way, in any of its forms, is not comprised of devotion. On this path, I set everything down, I hold nothing back, only God remains and that is complete."

Such is our intention.

Your initiatory project—that of your individuality, that of your community—must never lose sight of this goal. Each gesture must be incorporated in the final perspective of *Reintegration* or *awakening.*

In your actions, you must distinguish logical levels, the exoteric, the cultural, and the therapeutic (alignment of speech, thought, and action, reestablishment of the congruence between body, emotion, and thought), the mesoteric (self-remembering, presence in oneself, non-identification), the esoteric (subscription to the verticality that "I am That which remains, Absolute Will").

As seekers, you must focus your efforts on the mesoteric, that is, on accessing the real, and you should be uncompromising towards yourselves.

In terms of the exoteric, you must develop the greatest possible versatility. You will conquer the Solar Hierophany on the axis of the Real in order to apply it by radiance to the horizontal nature of the world and of worlds

Although we have tried to describe the following practices as clearly as possible, a transmission of the form by an experienced practitioner is indispensable.

Practice of the Division of Attention

This practice is the matrix of the three other fundamental practices. In each of the three other practices, in fact, the division of attention[120] will be present. More specifically, the precise realization of the three other practices necessitates the division of attention.

What is the problem set that prevails in the division of atten-

---

120   In previous editions of this text, we spoke of the division of consciousness rather than attention. It is a question of dividing objective consciousness, oriented towards the object, between several sensory objects. However, consciousness is always one. In order to avoid any confusion we have therefore opted for the more precise expression, division of attention.

tion? We do not live in the world but in its representation. We do not have access to pure experience and thus to reality; for the most part, we do not even have access to pure sensory experience. We are lived by our conditioning and we are held in the net of mental illusions. This representation is born of the process of identification led by analytical thought (which is sequential in nature).

Our everyday world, which we take for reality, is a dreamlike architecture maintained by pure convention. We could call this world a coherent field of representations. The inner dialogue holds this coherence together. If we stop the inner dialogue, we stop the representation, we stop the world, we can thus shift to the Real. The initiatory work begins with Silence, with the ability to stop the inner dialogue. For this, the practice of remembering oneself through the division of attention remains the most effective method. This consists of replacing analytical thought with the simultaneous perception of the world through the senses— ceasing to think about the world in order to perceive it.

Here is the protocol:

The practice can be done in stillness or in motion. At first, practice in a posture of your choosing that does not encourage sleep. After three months, it will be necessary to begin the practice in motion. You can practice the division of attention anytime, anywhere, during any human activity.

In the first three months, work at regular hours, three times a day, for three periods of about ten minutes each. Subsequently, work every time you think of it.

First, bring awareness to the overall posture of the body, from the feet on the ground to the top of the head.

At the same time, be simultaneously aware of the feeling inside your left hand. We will call this latter sensation the reference.

Your attention is thus divided in two. In the field of attention, there is posture and reference, simultaneously.

Then add the awareness of breath to this dual sensory perception.

Your attention is thus divided into three. In the field of attention, there is, simultaneously, posture, reference, and breath, three sensory objects.

The work actually begins here—that is to say, at the moment in which attention is divided into thirds.

You will, of course, be unable to maintain this simultaneous perception of posture, reference and breath. Thoughts will intervene. This is of no import. Every time you notice that you are newly mired in thought, return to your perceptions, always beginning with the reference. **You must remember yourself.** If you become submerged in the inner dialogue a thousand times, the key is to remember yourself a thousand and one times.

It will take several months until you imperfectly master this practice. Beginning in the first few weeks, however, you will notice significant changes in your life: greater control, less weariness, more substance, increased energy, an improved outlook on life, a heightened intensity.

The practice will progressively become an unconscious and automatic one; that is to say, it will exist on its own. Although here we call the memory of the body the "unconscious," this has nothing to do with the unconscious mind of psychoanalysis.

You will now be able to divide attention into four parts: posture, reference, breath, and wall of vision.

The wall of vision consists of an unfocused view. The broad gaze does not seek to deal with a particular point of the image, but rather to contemplate, generally, the wall of vision as perceived inside the head and not in some external place.

This practice often leads to slightly strange sensory experiences. You will then discover what Harding terms *the man with no head.* The coherence of the field of representation can indeed be modified. This coherence is built from a sort of gravitational center of representations. A shift in the center of gravity causes dramatic shifts to another coherence, and thus to another world.

You will need to practice this division of attention into four at length before moving on to the division of attention into five, adding the perception of the stream of sound. We then forget the vision to be attentive to the world of sound. The attention is thus divided into four: posture, reference, breath and the stream of sound.

As for the wall of vision, you will need to become aware of the stream of sound in its entirety, without an "auditory direction." Let the sounds seep in without processing them as pieces of information.

After several months of training in the quaternary division of attention, in its two forms (with the wall of vision or with the stream of sound), division of the attention into five, an exercise of great difficulty will be much more approachable.

The objective is not that you succeed in this division but that you practice these exercises. To stop the inner dialogue will at first become possible, then will later be relatively easy, before becoming totally natural.

Some adepts increase the division of attention to as many as seven parts by adding smell and taste. Experience shows that it is not necessary to do this as an exercise. When the division of attention into four is in place, smell and taste develop remarkably. We then find that many of our decisions that we think are reasoned and reasonable are dictated by the subtle play of smells that works intensely below the threshold of consciousness (remember the power of the smell of the bear).

You might feel that the inner dialogue has stopped, although you are in fact merely in a state of torpor. The division of attention is always accompanied by a **heightened consciousness.**

As soon as you become familiar with this practice, you will be able to participate in blind walks, which profoundly alter our sensory perceptions.

Our job is to move from having/doing to being, from analytical thinking to perceptual "thinking," from deep subjectivity to sensory objectivity, and to take on a "posture of being" through self-recollection that allows the *Presence* to take hold.

We will also note that this work leads to the definition of a Meta-Time or a Time of Times, a sacred interval in which the adept, like the artist, operates.

Let us reiterate that this propædeutic is the key to any real path. No theurgy, no alchemy can be realized within representation. It would then be only a dream within a dream, an illusion within the illusion. Theurgy and alchemy only have meaning within the Real, that is to say, within the "more-than-human states."

"Pure is he who dwells without thought."

"The sage does not think."

Meditation on the Letter A

This basic practice is common to Eastern and Western traditions. It makes up the central aspect of mantric practices with the root sounds **I, A,** and **O.**

The I is masculine, Yang; the O is feminine, Yin; and the **A** is androgynous. The letter **A** is at the origin of all Essences. As soon as you open your mouth, you emit the **A** sound. The letter **A** is the seedling of all phonemes, the mother of all letters.

A is both a symbol of beginning and of no production. Just as the **A** is present in all letters and contains them all, as a principle, so are all degrees of Realization, of Enlightenment, contained in the former, which is also the latter.

A is both being and non-being, and is thus the state beyond being and non-being: **A** is the Absolute.

In many secret schools, there is an alchemical interpretation of the **A,** most notably in the field of the internal alchemies of the Body of Glory. **A** corresponds to the two masculine and feminine principles brought together by the process of fusion, or the **A** even represents the Substantial state (substance of the heavens), where the Form and the Spirit merge, at the "unique point" of the Interval (the lightning bolt). The breath of the organs during this fusion is thus the breath of the original Awakening, without a beginning.

Liminal Practice

In a posture that ensures the spine's verticality, visualize a silver full Moon about five feet away from you, and a second silver-colored moon in your body, between the navel and the space of the heart.

Then, follow this protocol:

Inhale. Visualize the silver light leaving the outer Moon from the top in order to enter the inner Moon from above. At the same time, mentally produce the A sound.

Exhale. Visualize the silver light that leaves the inner Moon from the bottom in order to enter the outer Moon from below. At the same time, mentally produce the A sound.

Practice for approximately 20 minutes.

You will notice that this practice makes you divide attention into three: visualization, sound, and breath.

Once you are familiar with this stage, you will be able to add the reference (the inside of the palm of the hand, or the top of the skull).

This practice can be done at any given moment. It is advised that you practice in the evening at bedtime, so that you can continue it until the moment you fall asleep.

After one year of practicing this liminal form, you will be able to proceed to the inspection of the Letter A.

Inspection of the Letter A

This meditation is done on a full white Moon in which an eight-petaled rose blooms, and on which a golden letter **A** appears.

You can use calligraphy of Aleph, Greek or Arabic, or a Sanskrit or Tibetan A.

The Rose represents the eight dimensions of the Great Alchemical Work. In an ancient Greek tradition, a woman named *Octop* represents it. She also symbolizes the Heart and the Spirit.

Hang up the image that you have constructed and painted on a dark background on the wall—the Moon should have a diameter of 13 inches.

Sit down, facing the image, about five feet away.

Place the tongue against the palate.

The Inspection of letter A is done in three parts:

1.   While contemplating the Moon, the **A** sound is vibrated with each inhalation and exhalation.

2.   In the chest, at the level of the heart, create a Moon with the flower and the **A**, identical to the external image.

      The **A** sound is vibrated with the exhalation, while watching the energy leave the wheel of the inner Moon from the bottom and head towards the wheel of the outer Moon, thus bringing the image of **A** to life.

      The **A** sound is vibrated with the inhalation, while watching the energy leave the outer Moon from the top and enter the inner Moon from the top, to bring the image of **A** to life.

3.   Internal inspection. Work solely on the inner moon, as in phase 1.

A practice lasts at least 20 minutes. As soon as the practitioner is well acquainted with a phase, he can begin the second in this manner: phase 1 for 5 minutes and then phase 2. Later: phase 1, 5 minutes, phase 2, 10 minutes, then phase 3.

After a few weeks of practice, it will be easy to hold the outer Moon and the **A**, at the same time as the internal Moon and the **A**, through visualization and without external support.

The goal is to achieve the Inspection developed from the **A**, that is to say, a permanent practice everywhere, during any activity... without external support, as in the liminal practice. The adept is thus no longer the agent of the practice, but a witness to the practice.

This allows the practitioner to inscribe each of his gestures, each of his thoughts, in the **A** and thus in the breath of the universe. This is of the utmost importance in ritual celebration. All ritual should be recorded entirely in conscious breath.

The practice of the Letter **A** additionally allows the attainment of clarity within the dream. After a long period of work, the practitioner can even attempt the practice of the Letter **A** when falling asleep. He will quickly regain memories of dreams, then a clarification of those dreams, before being able to guide and master his oneiric activity, thanks to consciousness in the dream. This continuity of consciousness between dreams and wakefulness allows for the understanding that dreams and wakefulness are of the same nature and that, consequently, the Real is *different.*

A more advanced practice of the Letter **A** makes use of a rose with thirteen petals and the image of a double **A**, one red and one white, positioned to mirror one another.

The most accomplished form of the practice of the Letter **A** is that of the indistinguishable white **A**, on a limitless white background. This is the resulting form of the integration of the colorful letters **A**. In the field of internal alchemy, the practice of the white **A** corresponds to the final phase of the Work.

Practice of the I, A, O Sounds

The practice of the sounds **IAO** has two forms, one of them dynamic, densifying, that gathers energy, and the other harmonizing, a regulator of energies. The first form is recommended before operating, the second before a reconciliatory phase or rest.

A—Energizing practice.

The posture of work is the standing posture, without tension.

The complete cycle follows three breaths: Each breath has a corresponding sound, gesture, and perception.

Exhale deeply, completely emptying the lungs. Inhale through the nose while mentally producing the **E**[121] sound.

Exhale through the mouth while producing the **I** sound out loud and making the corresponding gesture with the right hand (index finger raised) in front of the throat. Attention is placed at the base of the skull.

Inhale while mentally producing the **E** sound.

Exhale while producing the **A** sound out loud and making the corresponding gesture of the right hand (open hand, thumb squared) in front of the heart. Attention is placed at the space of the heart.

Inhale while mentally producing the **E** sound.

Exhale through the mouth while producing the **O** sound out loud and making the corresponding gesture of the right hand (O is formed with the thumb and the index fingers) in front of the belly. Attention is placed three finger-widths below the navel, in the ocean of energy.

Throughout this whole cycle, the right hand gives and takes energy.

Repeat the cycle thusly for approximately five minutes, speed-

---

121   Short *e,* as in g*e*t.

ing up its rhythm.

Stop. Place your right hand in your left hand as if you were holding an egg. Press both hands beneath the navel and massage gently for one minute. Stop. Stay still while feeling the flow of energy.

Repeat this set three times. Each time, the process of speeding up will be increasingly important.

After the third time, proceed to the creation of the energetic sphere, whose center is the ocean of energy.

For this, proceed to four rotations in each plane—twelve rotations—always starting from the left (as a simple convention), two to the left, two to the right.

The practitioner is then the center of his own sphere of energy, and wherever he may go, he will remain at the center. Any theurgic operation will therefore take place from the center of the sphere and within the sphere. The practitioner thus remains along this axis.

B—Harmonizing practice.

The working posture is the posture called the equestrian-archer; you sit in the empty space as if you were on horseback. The pelvis therefore tilts forward without tension, allowing the spinal column to effortlessly remain straight. This posture is closer to the listening posture of Dr. Tomatis. Note that any hieratic posture allows the establishment of this energetic axis.

The complete cycle follows four breaths:

Hands are on the belly, fingers folded over each other.

Inhale through the nose while mentally producing the E sound and moving your hands up to the throat.

Turn your head to the left and slowly open the left hand, as if bending a bow on your left side. The right hand remains in front of the throat. Exhale through the mouth simultaneously while producing the I sound out loud.

Inhale while mentally producing the E sound and bringing the left hand back towards the right, in front of the throat. Return your gaze in front of you.

Move your hands down toward the ocean of energy of the belly while producing the O sound out loud as you exhale.

Inhale anew while mentally producing the E sound and moving your hands up to your heart.

Turn your head to the right and slowly open the right hand, as if bending a bow on your right side. Simultaneously exhale while audibly producing the A sound.

Inhale while mentally producing the E sound and bringing the right hand towards the left, in front of the heart. Return your gaze in front of you.

Move your hands down toward the ocean of energy of the belly while producing the O sound out loud as you exhale.

Repeat this cycle three times.

Stay in the silence of perception.

Meditation of Infinity in the Body

PRELIMINARY EXPLANATIONS BY JEAN-PIERRE KRASENSKY.

The Primary Respiratory Mechanism (PRM) is a fluctuation of Cerebrospinal Fluid (CSF).

CSF is a liquid in which the brain and spinal cord are immersed. It is also found along the nerve sheaths that run through the body.

CSF is formed in the head, from arterial blood in the brain's ventricles. It passes from one ventricle to another, moving down the length of the meninges that surround the spinal cord, primarily the arachnoid mater, and circulates throughout the whole body. The lymph is formed from this very liquid, which then returns to the vena cava, and to the heart and the arteries. The circle is complete.

CSF is imbued with a rhythmic movement of unknown origin. The osteopaths, Sutherland being the first, called this rhythmic movement the Primary Respiratory Mechanism. The CSF thus has a rhythmic movement that makes it descend and ascend, a motion called flexion/extension, which is more accurate than describing a descent and an ascent.

PRM fills all body parts with its rhythm, except the heel bone, the calcaneus, which does not fluctuate. It essentially works as a support base on the ground when walking, and must therefore remain stable.

All bones fluctuate based on this pace of flexion/extension. The movements are faint, but they give life to the body. The rate of this fluctuation is 6 to 8 cycles per minute.

In order to regulate this movement, the human body makes use of three primary anatomical pivots: the cuboid at the foot, the sacrum at the pelvis, and the occiput at the head. These three bones have a synchronized collective movement. In fact, the cuboid (the earth), the sacrum (which links the earth to the heavens, the base of sacred ascent), and the occiput (the sky) are the regulating pivots of the PRM that set the pace for all fluctuations of the body—physical, organic, hormonal, psychological, etc.

PRM is related to the pulmonary function. When pulmonary respiration takes on the same pace as the PRM, we find ourselves in a state of hypnosis or meditation, and then sleep. When we accelerate the pace of the PRM and that of pulmonary respiration, we reach a trance-like state or one of orgasm.

PRM comes into existence before pulmonary respiration, since it is present before childbirth and remains after death.

PRM and Tradition

Many traditions mention the equivalent of PRM. Taoism is one example of this.

In internal Taoist alchemy, some exercises involve transmuting *Jing,* the primordial energy, into *Qi,* nourishing breath—then turning the *Qi* into *Shen,* spiritual energy, and finally the *Shen* into vacuity. These Taoist exercises are practiced based on a microcosmic cycle that borrows the paths of the governor and conception meridians, to create an ascent and descent of breath, and thus a flexion/extension that requires the synchronous mobilization of the sacrum and the occiput identical to that of the PRM.

It must be noted that this cycle—which follows a defined rhythm, is not immutable in time, does not exist in the universal principle—makes it possible to move from the tangible world (sky, occiput, *Shen*) through an intermediary stage (sacrum balance point, *Qi*). Man is indeed a mediator between earth and the heavens.

Similar exercises can be found in Tantra, but also in Chaldeo-Egyptian or Pythagorean schools. This microcosmic circulation is the internal, intra-corporeal representation (the projection or the precipitation) to which it is intimately linked.

Some adepts in antiquity knew what we have called the Primary Respiratory Mechanism since the beginning of the 20th century.

The practice

The goal in this practice is to become aware of the inscription of the rhythm of the universe, the *breath of the universe,* within ourselves. In a way, it is becoming aware that the universe *meditates* in us, and that it is therefore enough to become aware of the "meditation of the infinite in the body."

For this, we will start with an artificial practice that will allow us to "affix" this internal rhythm.

Assume a posture that allows a correct placement of the spine.

Adhere to the following protocol. Move to the next step only when you have mastered the preceding one.

- *Step 1:*

Become aware of a point at the base of the occiput.

With this point, trace, with a very slight oscillation, the sign of infinity:

Completely let yourself go in this movement, without controlling anything, such that the movement synchronizes itself with the breath.

- *Step 2:*

Move the "drawing point" forward inside the head. The oscillatory movement is then felt inside the head. After a moment, you must perceive the movement, all while remaining motionless.

- *Step 3:*

Begin to perceive this oscillation during your activities.

- *Step 4:*

Lower the oscillation along the spinal column to the level of the heart.

Feel the movement well.

- *Step 5:*

Lower the oscillation along the spinal column to the ocean of energy (two finger-widths below the navel).

Feel the movement well.

- *Step 6:*

Lower the oscillation along the spinal column to the sacrum.

Feel the movement well.

- *Step 7:*

Let the movement invade the body. This step must emerge automatically and not be sought.

You can then seek to focus the movement on an organ or on one part of the body in order to eliminate toxins or other impurities.

Four Make One

The four techniques are in fact a single technique. Each of these exercises conceals another that you will discover little by little.

When these four techniques are mastered, that is to say, in the memory of the body, you can combine them, first 2 by 2, then 3 by 3, and finally unify them into a single technique that will become a way of life.

There are many variants of this first quadrant of awakening, which is in the modality of forms. The second quadrant of awakening, which emerges from the first, is in the modality of energies. Finally, the third quadrant of awakening is the modality of essences.

Verify that the practice is accurate.
The verification of a real practice is always behavioral:
- control of the environment.
- the art of "bending" time.
- development of energy and *solarity*.
- greater serenity. "Keep calm!"

Here are some criteria, among others, that will allow you to know if you are on the right track.

Remember:

The division of attention leads to **Heightened consciousness.**

The practice of Letter A leads to **Vacuity.**

The practice of Sounds leads to the **Mastery of the power of creation.**

The practice of Meditation of Infinity in the Body leads to **Fusion.**

All of this, through presence Here and Now, allows for **Autonomy.**

Autonomy, according to its etymology, *autosnomos,* means **"he who gives himself his own law."** This indicates the exit from the circle of identifications, dilutions, representations and mental crystallizations, to reach the Center where simply "I am" or "I remain"; no longer "being lived" to live; to become truly "alive." It is only in the Center that we can give ourselves our own laws, so that we can be autonomous.

Gnostic Way of Panaghion:[122] First station

Rules:

This practice is reserved for those familiar with the practice of the four basic techniques.

Whenever it is not specified, consciousness is at the top of the skull, at the fontanel.

Consciousness always descends on the exhalations and always rises on the inhalations, in the center of the spine. Consciousness is placed in the center of the spine in the front of the central channel for the exhalation and at the back of the central channel for the inhalation. The energy centers are perceived in the void of the central channel.

Move from one posture to another on a retention of breath at the end of the inhalation, placing awareness at the top of the head.

Exhale when the next posture is adopted.

Take a normal, calm breath before starting the next exercise.

Except for the practice of IAO, the tongue is naturally slightly rolled back, the tip touching the middle of the palate. "Naturally" means not willed. This position of the tongue is achieved effortlessly when the tongue, the cheeks, and the back of the throat are relaxed. The tongue then "falls" backwards, the tip pointing to the awareness at the top of the head.

A—Salutations facing East

Standing.
Legs slightly bent.
Pelvis slightly tilted forward.
Chin slightly tucked in.
Hands crossed over the heart.

---

122 *Panaghion,* initiatory name of Armand Toussaint.

Awareness at the top of the head (fontanel).

Feel the throbbing or vibration.

Breathe consciously.

Hold the breath at the top of the head at the end of an inhalation.

Get on your knees.

Bend your forehead towards the floor.

Exhale while tucking in your chin. Breathe normally.

Hold the breathe at the end of an inhalation.

Get up. Exhale.

Perform this greeting three times.

Remain standing in silence. Awareness at the top of yourself.

B—Meditation of Infinity in the body

AWARENESS OF THE CENTERS THROUGH BREATHING

Standing or sitting.

Posture adapted to the practice, but comfortable.

The eyes are closed. The eyebrows up.

Place awareness at the back of the neck (the point of the witness).

Enter the **Head Center** (corresponding to the pituitary gland).

Feel the oscillation. Breathe calmly.

Climb to the **Crown Center, at the top of the head** on a deep inhalation.

Feel the oscillation. Breathe calmly.

From the top of the head, **lower awareness to the Head Center** on an exhalation. Go back to the top of the head on the inhalation (3 times).

From the top of the head, **lower awareness to the Throat Center** on an exhalation. Go back to the top of the head on the inhalation (3 times).

From the top of the head, **lower awareness to the Heart Center** on an exhalation. Go back to the top of the head on the inhalation (3 times).

From the top of the head, **lower awareness to the Solar Plexus Center** on an exhalation. Go back to the top of the head on the inhalation (3 times).

From the top of the head, **lower awareness to the Navel Center** on an exhalation (two fingers under the navel, in the spine). Go back to the top of the head on the inhalation (3 times).

From the top of the head, **lower awareness to the Sexual Center** (four fingers above the base of the spine, in the spine) on an exhalation. Go back to the top of the head on the inhalation (3 times).

From the top of the head, **lower awareness to the Root Center** (located at the base of the spine) on an exhalation. Go back to the top of the head on the inhalation (3 times).

Remain aware of the oscillation at the top of the head and let it radiate throughout the body from this point of infinity.

Normal breathing.

C—IAO Practice, Solar Form (See *The Quadrant of Awakening*)

Practice IAO in its solar form 3 times: very slowly, slowly, quickly.

D—Practice of the Letter A (See *The Quadrant of Awakening*)

The eyes are open. Defocused gaze.
Deep practice.

E—Energy sequence

Five stretches that redeploy energy in the body.
Do the sequence 1, 3, 7, or more times.
Standing facing North.

Feet spread shoulder width apart.
Legs slightly bent.

Close your fists and bend your arms to place your fists under your armpits.

Inhale deeply. Exhale as you bend to your left.

Rise up on the inhalation.

Exhale as you bend to your right.

Rise up on the inhalation.

Exhale as you bend forward to look between your legs.

Rise up on the inhalation.

Cross your hands behind your back, raise your crossed hands as high as possible, going up towards the back of your neck.

Exhale as you lean back as far as possible.

Rise up on the inhalation.

Place your hands on the hips, as if to contain the belly with your fingers.

Lunge forward on the left leg.

Lower yourself as much as possible by bending the left knee, back straight, looking to the horizon, expelling air, and tucking your belly in.

Raise up slightly and slowly pivot while inhaling.

You are now in a right forward lunge.

Lower yourself as much as possible by bending the left knee, back straight, looking to the horizon, expelling air, and tucking your belly in.

Slowly straighten up while inhaling, still in a forward lunge.

Place awareness on top of the head.

Roll your head in a circular motion.

Straighten up slowly while inhaling, face north, put feet together, drop arms.

Breathe normally.

Let the energy radiate throughout the body.

F—Panaghion Meditation

Seated.

Posture adapted to the practice, but comfortable.

The eyes are closed. The eyebrows up.

☙ SEQUENCE OF DESCENDING BREATH

Place **awareness at the back of the neck** (the point of the witness).

Enter **the Head Center.**

Feel the oscillation. Breathe calmly.

Go up to **the Crown Center on a deep inhalation.**

Feel the oscillation. Breathe calmly.

From the top of the head, **lower awareness to the Head Center** on an exhalation.

Hold the breath for a few seconds without effort.

Go up to the top of the head on the inhalation.

Hold the breath for a few seconds without effort.

From the top of the head, **lower awareness to the Throat Center** on an exhalation.

Hold. Go back to the top of the head on the inhalation. Hold.

From the top of the head, **lower awareness to the Heart Center** on an exhalation.

Hold. Go back to the top of the head on the inhalation. Hold.

From the top of the head, **lower awareness to the Solar Plexus Center** on an exhalation.

Hold. Go back to the top of the head on the inhalation. Hold.

From the top of the head, **lower awareness to the Navel Center** on an exhalation.

Hold. Go back to the top of the head on the inhalation. Hold.

From the top of the head, **lower awareness to the Sexual Center** on an exhalation.

Hold. Go back to the top of the head on the inhalation. Hold.

From the top of the head, **lower awareness to the Root Center** on an exhalation.

Hold. Go back to the top of the head on the inhalation. Hold.

☙ SEQUENCE OF ASCENDING BREATH

From the top of the head, **lower awareness to the Root Center** on an exhalation.

Hold. Go back to the top of the head on the inhalation. Hold.

From the top of the head, **lower awareness to the Sexual Center** on an exhalation.

Hold. Go back to the top of the head on the inhalation. Hold.

From the top of the head, **lower awareness to the Navel Center** on an exhalation.

Hold. Go back to the top of the head on the inhalation. Hold.

From the top of the head, **lower awareness to the Solar Plexus Center** on an exhalation.

Hold. Go back to the top of the head on the inhalation. Hold.

From the top of the head, **lower awareness to the Heart Center** on an exhalation.

Hold. Go back to the top of the head on the inhalation. Hold.

From the top of the head, **lower awareness to the Throat Center** on an exhalation.

Hold. Go back to the top of your head on the inhalation. Hold.

From the top of the head, **lower awareness to the Head Center** on an exhalation.

Hold. Go back to the top of the head on the inhalation. Hold.

Remain aware of the oscillation at the top of the head and allow it to radiate throughout the body from this point of infinity.

Normal breathing.

You can repeat this sequence of descent and ascent of the breath.

From the top of the head, exhale deeply.

Hold. Go up above the top of the head on the inhalation.

Breathe normally.

Remain in the fullness of Silence and the Void.

G—Practice of IAO, Lunar or Harmonizing Form (See *The Quadrant of Awakening*)

Practice IAO in this form 3 times, very slowly.

H—Practice of the Letter A (See *The Quadrant of Awakening*)

The eyes are open.

Defocused gaze.

I—Final bow facing East

Standing.

Legs slightly bent.

Pelvis slightly tilted forward. Chin slightly tucked in.

Hands crossed over the heart.

Awareness at the top of the head (fontanel).

Feel the throbbing or vibration.

Breathe consciously.

Hold the breath at the top of the head at the end of an inhalation.

Kneel.

Bend your forehead towards the floor.

Exhale while tucking in your chin.

Breathe normally. Hold the breathe at the end of an inhalation.

Get up.

Exhale.

Remain standing in silence. Awareness at the top of yourself.

Gnostic Way of Panaghion: Second station

The second station is almost identical to the first station with inversions on some exercises between the inhalation and the exhalation which cause a variation of the movement of the serpentine energies.

For practical reasons, however, we repeat all the exercises even when they are identical.

Rules:

This practice is reserved for those who are familiar with the practice of the four basic techniques and the first station of the Gnostic Way of Panaghion.

Whenever it is not specified, awareness is at the top of the head, at the fontanel.

Awareness always rises on the exhalation and always descends on the inhalation (unlike the first station) in the center of the spine. Awareness is placed in the center of the spine at the front of the central channel for the inhalation and at the back of the central channel for the exhalation. The energy centers are perceived in the void of the central channel.

We go from one posture to another on a holding of the breath at the end of the exhalation with awareness at the top of the skull.

We inhale when the following posture is adopted.

One takes a normal and calm breath before starting the next exercise.

Except for the practice of IAO, the tongue is naturally slightly rolled back, the tip touching the middle of the palate. "Naturally" means not willed. This position of the tongue is achieved effortlessly when the tongue, the cheeks, and the back of the throat are relaxed. The tongue then "falls" backwards, the tip pointing to the awareness at the top of the head.

A—Salutations facing East

Standing.

Legs slightly bent.

Pelvis slightly tilted forward.

Chin slightly tucked in.

Hands crossed over the heart.

Awareness at the top of the head (fontanel).

Feel the throbbing or vibration.

Breathe consciously.

Hold the breath at the top of the head at the end of an inhalation.

Get on your knees.

Bend your forehead towards the floor.

Exhale while tucking in your chin. Breathe normally.

Hold the breath at the end of an inhalation.

Get up. Exhale.

Perform this greeting three times.

Remain standing in silence. Awareness at the top of yourself.

B—Meditation of Infinity in the body

AWARENESS OF THE CENTERS THROUGH BREATHING

Standing or sitting.

Posture adapted to the practice, but comfortable.

The eyes are closed. The eyebrows up.

Place awareness at the back of the neck (the point of the witness).

Enter the **Head Center** (corresponding to the pituitary gland).

Feel the oscillation. Breathe calmly.

Climb to the **Crown Center, at the top of the head** on a deep exhalation.

Feel the oscillation. Breathe calmly.

From the top of the head, **lower awareness to the Head Center** on an inhalation. Go back to the top of the head on the exhalation (3 times).

From the top of the head, **lower awareness to the Throat Center** on an inhalation. Go back to the top of the head on the exhalation (3 times).

From the top of the head, **lower awareness to the Heart Center** on an inhalation. Go back to the top of the head on the exhalation (3 times).

From the top of the head, **lower awareness to the Solar Plexus Center** on an inhalation. Go back to the top of the head on the exhalation (3 times).

From the top of the head, **lower awareness to the Navel Center** on an inhalation (two fingers under the navel, in the spine). Go back to the top of the head on the exhalation (3 times).

From the top of the head, **lower awareness to the Sexual Center** (four fingers above the base of the backbone, in the spine) on an inhalation. Go back to the top of the head on the exhalation (3 times).

From the top of the head, **lower awareness to the Root Center** (located at the very base of the spine) on an inhalation. Go back to the top of the head on the exhalation (3 times).

Remain aware of the oscillation at the top of the head and let it radiate throughout the body from this point of infinity.

Normal breathing.

C—IAO Practice, Solar Form (See *The Quadrant of Awakening*)

Practice IAO in its solar form 3 times, very slowly, slowly, quickly.

D—Practice of the Letter A (See *The Quadrant of Awakening*)

The eyes are open. Defocused gaze.
Deep practice.

E—Energy sequence

Five stretches that redeploy energy in the body.
Do the sequence 1, 3, 7, or more times.
Standing facing North.
>Feet spread shoulder width apart.
>Legs slightly bent.

Close your fists and bend your arms to place your fists under your armpits.

Inhale deeply. Exhale as you bend to your left.
Rise up on the inhalation.
Exhale as you bend to your right.
Rise up on the inhalation.
Exhale as you bend forward to look between your legs.
Rise up on the inhalation.

Cross your hands behind your back, raise your crossed hands as high as possible, going up towards the back of your neck.

Exhale as you lean back as far as possible.
Rise up on the inhalation.

Place your hands on the hips, as if to contain the belly with your fingers.

Lunge forward on the left leg.

Lower yourself as much as possible by bending the left knee, back straight, looking to the horizon, expelling air, and tucking your belly in.

Raise up slightly and slowly pivot while inhaling.

You are now in a right forward lunge.

Lower yourself as much as possible by bending the left knee, back straight, looking to the horizon, expelling air, and tucking your belly in.

Straighten up slowly while inhaling, still in a forward lunge.

Place awareness on top of the head.

Roll your head in a circular motion.

Straighten up slowly while inhaling, face north, put feet together, drop arms.

Breathe normally.

Let the energy radiate throughout the body.

F—Panaghion Meditation

Seated.

Posture adapted to the practice, but comfortable.

The eyes are closed. The eyebrows up.

☙ SEQUENCE OF DESCENDING BREATH

Place **awareness at the back of the neck** (the point of the witness).

Enter **the Head Center.**

Feel the oscillation. Breathe calmly.

Go up to **the Crown Center** on a deep exhalation.

Feel the oscillation. Breathe calmly.

From the top of the head, **lower awareness to the Center of the head** on an inhalation.

Hold the breath for a few seconds without effort.

Go back to the top of the head on the exhalation.

Hold the breath for a few seconds without effort.

From the top of the head, **lower awareness to the Throat Center** on an inhalation.

Hold. Go back to the top of the head on the exhalation. Hold.

From the top of the head, **lower awareness to the Heart**

Center on an inhalation.

Hold. Go back to the top of the head on the exhalation. Hold.

From the top of the head, **lower awareness to the Solar Plexus Center** on an inhalation.

Hold. Go back to the top of the head on the exhalation. Hold.

From the top of the head, **lower awareness to the Navel Center** on an inhalation.

Hold. Go back to the top of the head on the exhalation. Hold.

From the top of the head, **lower awareness to the Sexual Center** on an inhalation.

Hold. Go back to the top of the head on the exhalation. Hold.

From the top of the head, **lower awareness to the Root Center** on an inhalation.

Hold. Go back to the top of the head on the exhalation. Hold.

☞ Sequence of ascending breath

From the top of the head, **lower awareness to the Root Center** on an inhalation.

Hold. Go back to the top of the head on the exhalation. Hold.

From the top of the head, **lower awareness to the Sexual Center** on an inhalation.

Hold. Go back to the top of the head on the exhalation. Hold.

From the top of the head, **lower awareness to the Navel Center** on an inhalation.

Hold. Go back to the top of the head on the exhalation. Hold.

From the top of the head, **lower awareness to the Solar Plexus Center** on an inhalation.

Hold. Go back to the top of the head on the exhalation. Hold.

From the top of the head, **lower awareness to the Heart Center** on an inhalation.

Hold. Go back to the top of the head on the exhalation. Hold.

From the top of the head, **lower awareness to the Throat**

Center on an inhalation.

Hold. Go back to the top of the head on the exhalation. Hold.

From the top of the head, **lower awareness to the Head Center** on an inhalation.

Hold. Go back to the top of the head on the exhalation. Hold.

Remain aware of the oscillation at the top of the head and allow it to radiate throughout the body from this point of infinity.

Normal breathing.

You can repeat this sequence of descent and ascent of the breath.

From the top of the head, exhale deeply.

Hold. Go up above the top of the head on the inhalation.

Breathe normally.

Remain in the fullness of Silence and the Void.

G—Practice of IAO, Lunar or Harmonizing Form (See *The Quadrant of Awakening*)

Practice IAO in this form 3 times, very slowly.

H—Practice of the Letter A (See *The Quadrant of Awakening*)

The eyes are open.

Defocused gaze.

I—Final bow facing East

Standing.

Legs slightly bent.

Pelvis slightly tilted forward. Chin slightly tucked in.

Hands crossed over the heart.

Awareness at the top of the head (fontanel).

Feel the throbbing or vibration.

Breathe consciously.

Hold the breath at the top of the head at the end of an exhalation.

Kneel.

Bend your forehead towards the floor.

Exhale while tucking in your chin.

Breathe normally. Hold the breath at the end of an exhalation.

Get up.

Exhale.

Remain standing in silence. Awareness at the top of yourself.

The Chivalric Way

Armand Toussaint[123] attributed to the cloak the same symbolic value as the knight's armor, which was for him of an energetic nature. He often referred to the armor and helmet of Athena, the material of which, he said, is that energy generated by the full activity of the energy centers in the body, or chakras. We find in classical Christian iconography, Catholic or Orthodox, many indications of how to constitute this armor or cloak. The concept developed by Armand Toussaint is reminiscent of certain martial traditions that develop a cloak of energy capable of absorbing blows and even returning the destructive effects on the opponent.

But it was to the kabbalah taught by his master, Serge Marcotoune of Kiev, that Armand Toussaint referred in order to constitute the twenty-two pieces of armor.

In a table, Armand Toussaint wanted both to synthesize the mantric practice, based here on Hebrew, but which finds its equivalent in Latin or ancient Greek, which allows the development of the armor, or cloak, and to summarize the alchemical process that leads to the Great Work. These are simple indications for a grand design.

---

123 Armand Toussaint (1895-1994), eminent figure of the Martinist scene, was the founder and head of the *Ordre Martiniste des Chevaliers du Christ* from 1971, when it was founded, until his death in 1994.

Alpha: "Know thyself..."

The initiate seeks his Unknown within himself.

Aleph	1	The will of unity (Alchemical Salt)
Beth	2	The science of the inner binary
Gimel	3	The positive inner synthesis
Daleth	4	The quaternary of realization: *Sta—Solve—Coagula—Multiplica*
He	5	The inspired will, the era of the Popes
Vav	6	The choice of the Path between spiritual Clarity and Darkness
Zain	7	The triumph or failure of spirit over matter
Cheth	8	The search and acquisition of inner balance
Teth	9	The integration of enriching experiences through mystical techniques: *Look to see—Listen to hear—Make the inner Silence: "Vide, Audi, Tace"*

Delta: "...you will know the others..."

The initiate in manifestation in the world, his habits and customs, learns to live there by experiencing the attacks that strengthen him. He dwells in the world, but he does not identify with the world, nor with worlds.

Yod	10	The time, the opportunity to experiment in the vortices of the world.
Kaph	11 or 20	The occult force.

Lamed .... 12 or 30 .... The sacrifice that the initiate makes by accepting constraints to make them serve his spiritual progression.

Mem .... 13 or 40 .... The conquest of death or the division of consciousness, the change of dimension (Alchemical Sulfur).

Nun .... 14 or 50 .... Energetic recapitulation, new associations, the creation of a favorable future karma.

Samekh .... 15 or 60 .... The attack of Baphomet, emotional reactions.

A'in .... 16 or 70 .... The shelter or the ruin.

Pe .... 17 or 80 .... The star of hope.

Tzadi .... 18 or 90 .... The disappointment caused by treacherous attacks.

Omega: "...and the Gods."

The initiate projects his love of the Beautiful, the True, and the Good into the world.

Qoph .... 19 or 100 ...... The inner light has come into being by the inner silence.

Resh.............. 20 or 200 ..... Time, Rebirth, Renewal, Longevity, Immortality.

Shin .... 21 or 300 ...... Victory in the very Kingdom of the Prince of this world. The Initiate, Fool of Spiritual Light, pursues his Way in his mystic intoxication, indifferent to the attacks of evil: he is the *Mat* in the Tarot of the visionaries of the Middle Ages, dead to the world.

Tav .... 22 or 400 ..... The Great Alchemical and Spiritual Work or the reward of the Man-God, replica of the God-Man, the New Man, Christ, the Panacea, the Philosopher's Stone.

Kaph final .... 23 or 500 ...... The active Will supported by experience and hope.

Mem final .... 24 or 600 ..... The second Death with penetration into the World of the Spirit by the judicious, liberated, and sacrificial choice. The double Essence.

Nun final ..... 25 or 700 ...... The triumphal Will, in the storm, to wash away the karma of the world (*peccata mundi*). The triple Essence.

Pe final .... 26 or 800 ..... The hope of redemption that induces spiritual balance in the world. The quadruple Essence.

Tzadi final ... 27 or 900 ..... The discovery of a great Synthesis. Higher Initiation of the Rose-Croix (or Bodhisattva). The Quintessence.

New Aleph ... 28 or 1000 ... Liberation. The birth of the creative sun. Unification in the Breast of God. The Reintegration of the Ascended Master. The Millennium.

Let us remember that the states mentioned above, places-states as Claude Bruley[124] would say, are not states of the "person," of the body-mind system, but of the differentiated states of increased consciousness in Silence. It is under the cloak of Silence that "the initiate seeks his Unknown within himself." In this path towards the One, we will note the initial importance of the will to unity, a will that we find active and then triumphant throughout the initiatory process.

This chivalric way requires a daily practice, a practice of re-membering oneself and the Self which can take many forms, but in which we will always find the same keys.

Here is one of the most direct forms. The steps are cumula-tive. Each step should be worked for about 10 days. Of course, there are days when you might not think about practicing, or you might think that you are not in the best condition to practice. By combining the exercises, some will be forgotten. It's all part of the process.

Note without judging your progress and difficulties that will gradually fade. The important thing, to use Louis-Claude de Saint-Martin's phrase, is to "hold on."

Alpha Phase:

• Step 1: At least seven[125] times a day, remember to physically stand up, looking far and wide.

• Step 2 (+ 1): At least seven times a day, breathe consciously, pay attention to the movement of the breath for a few minutes, to the inhalation, to the exhalation, and to the intervals between the

---

124 *Le Grand Œuvre comme fondement d'une spiritualité laïque. Le che-min de l'individuation,* by Claude Bruley (Cordes-sur-Ciel, Fr: Rafael de Surtis, 2008).

125 The number 7 is indicative. The goal is to think of self-remembering several times a day until it becomes natural.

inhalation and the exhalation, the exhalation and the inhalation.

• Step 3 (+ 1 and 2): At least seven times a day, watch your words. Think beforehand about what to say.

• Step 4 (+ 1, 2 and 3): At least seven times a day, observe your thoughts for a few minutes without judging.

Delta Phase:

• Step 5: At least seven times a day, look with completely new eyes at your surroundings, aware that what you are looking at is unique, and appears the moment you look at it. Become aware that this object (human being, animal, thing, event...) is made of all that it was and all that it will be until its disappearance. This object within your consciousness is of the nature of emptiness.

• Step 6: In the evening before going to bed, recap what you did and thought during the day in as much detail as possible, going back in time from the present moment. What did you do, say, or think just before you started the recap, then just before that and so on, until the time you woke up. Little by little, you will grasp that the present contains the totality of the past, yours and that of all beings.

• Step 7: Find out what form of death, of your own death, you absolutely dread and, three times a day, deliberately imagine that you will die thus. Feel physically and psychically all the horror of this dreaded death. Gradually, the deleterious effect will diminish until fear ceases to affect you.

Omega Phase:

• Step 8: Place your awareness, as often as possible, at the back of your head, about four inches behind and slightly above the back of the skull, where Christian iconography places the halo of saints. Observe the movements of your body and your psyche from this point, without judging. Realize that your "person," your "game," is an aggregate of heterogeneous elements without continuity.

• Step 9: Combine step 2 and step 8 as often as possible. This step can be extended indefinitely until you enter the Land of Silence.

• Step 10: Realize, as often as possible, that whatever is present, like whatever is absent, is within your consciousness. Nothing can be outside of your consciousness. You are the unique creator, producer, director, actor, and spectator of your consciousness which is none other than the original and ultimate consciousness. You are.

Conclusions

These three sets of spiritual exercises, the Quadrant of Awakening, the Way of Panaghion, and the Chivalric Way, may seem difficult. They are. It is not the perfection of the practice that promotes realization, but the practice itself. Moreover, the practice is the realization.

Rather than working to obtain, it is about working to celebrate what has already been there since the dawn of time. You are the Divine, and are so regardless of the conditions momentarily imposed by duality.

If you decide to practice, it is not to change anything in the world of form, but to manifest what you are, your original and ultimate nature. Changes will manifest, or not, in the peripheries of life. It is incidental. What is essential is the radiance of Being, in and beyond form.

These practices are not intended for permanent engagement. A breath between effort and non-effort allows the deep integration of what practice induces in the metaphysical order. It is up to each individual, possibly accompanied by an experienced practitioner, to feel which rhythm is most favorable to their psycho-physiological constitution.

Remember that the practices lead to the abandonment of all practices. However, we can only give up what we have.

Appendix 2

Armand Toussaint
A man out of the stream

Armand Toussaint (1895-1994) was one of the most astonishing and endearing figures of twentieth century Hermetism. He played a central but discreet and elegant role on the esoteric scene.

A former student of the Athénée Royal de Charleroi, where he studied science, Armand Toussaint worked all his professional life at SNCB, the Belgian National Railway Company, as a principal inspector, which allowed him to travel extensively and facilitated greatly the singular encounters that were decisive for his "career as a hermeticist," a career that we will summarize here.

Armand Toussaint and Rosicrucianism

Armand Toussaint was President of the Belgian branch of the Rosicrucian Fellowship of Max Heindel from 1933 to 1970. He separated from this organization, in disagreement with the dogmatism of those responsible for Oceanside, whom he most often described as "functionaries." In general, he always had to beware of the American tendency to transform a spiritual or initiatory school into a supermarket and fought against all dogmatic or totalitarian tendencies. It was therefore in April 1971 that he created the Rosicrucian Brotherhood which he presented as a continuation of Max Heindel's teaching. Until the end of his life, he maintained close relations with a former college of the Rose-Croix, remaining the Friend and Elder Brother of several of its members. He transmitted to the end an internal alchemy peculiar to this Rosicrucian current.

Armand Toussaint and the Gnostic Church

Armand Toussaint played an important role within the framework of Gnostic currents.[126] It was Roger Deschamps, departed for the Eternal Orient on December 23, 1964, who consecrated Armand Toussaint to the Episcopate on June 1, 1963, under the mystical name of Tau Raymond. Roger Deschamps was Bishop and Primate of Belgium in the Gnostic Apostolic Church. He himself had been consecrated by Robert Ambelain (John III) on May 31, 1959, under the name of Tau Jean Rudiger.[127] Later, André Mauer (Tau André), who succeeded Robert Ambelain as Patriarch of the Apostolic Gnostic Church, unwilling to form a highly cen-

---

126 Read on this subject *Qu'est-ce que l'Église Gnostique?* by Tau Jacques, a statement of the different historical branches of the Gnostic Church since its creation by Jules Doinel (Guérigny, Fr: CIREM, 1996).

127 We have not found an ordination certificate for Tau Jean Rudiger. The ordination is, however, attested.

tralized and administered Church, considered the Gnostic Bishops to be Free Bishops.

On several occasions, Armand Toussaint proposed to the Synod of the Apostolic Gnostic Church that it should abolish all segregation of sex in ordinations and, consequently, "admit women, all other conditions fulfilled, to the major degrees of Presbyter (Priest) and even Episcope (Bishop)."[128] Faced with the rejection of the Synod, Armand Toussaint founded in 1969 the Rosicrucian Apostolic Church, open equally to men and women, with an old fellow traveler and one of those he considered to be his "spiritual sons," Marcel Jirousek. The influence of the Rosicrucian Apostolic Church grew, from the second half of the 1980s to this day, thanks to the action of three personalities of the Hermetic scene: Charles-Rafael Payeur, Triantaphyllos Kotzamanis (T. Hieronymus) and T. Pol Lysis. The first, consecrated by Armand Toussaint in 1985, founded the Sacerdotal College of the Rose+Cross before joining the Catholic Apostolic Church of Brazil, not hostile to esotericists. Since then, Charles-Rafael Payeur has continued to develop a teaching, through courses, audio recordings, conferences, and books, where the occult blends into a deep humanism. Triantaphyllos Kotzamanis, who died prematurely during the night of 15-16 December 2007, responsible for the Great Adriatic Sanctuary in Greece and a principal figure of the Order of the Lily and Eagle, became Archbishop-Primate of Greece in the Rosicrucian Apostolic Church (called in Greece the Rosicrucian Gnostic & Apostolic Church). Kotzamanis fought for more than ten years for the legal recognition of this church in the face of the all-powerful hegemony of the Greek Orthodox Church, which saw there an attack on its "sovereignty." Triantaphyllos Kotzamanis won his case, defeating all expectations. T. Pol Lysis, Archbishop-Primate of France, Switzerland, and Italy,

---

128 Extract from a letter sent on April 8, 1972 to Roger Caro.

on the contrary, has preserved the discreet and esoteric character of the Church, which Armand Toussaint entrusted to him, by reserving it for Martinists, Rosicrucians, Pythagoreans, and Freemasons. Since the departure of Triantaphyllos Kotzamanis, the Rosicrucian Apostolic Church has been directed by a college. After a temporary externalization on an experimental basis, it has again been hidden but is not dormant, contrary to what is affirmed, not without malice, on the site of a recently created church that seeks to capture the Gnostic heritage of Armand Toussaint.

Today, the Rosicrucian Apostolic Church founded by Armand Toussaint is present discreetly on three continents and continues the work for which it was conceived by its founder for the benefit of the members of Freemasonry, Martinism, Rosicrucianism, and other traditional currents. It has developed particular expressions: Swedenborgian, Chinese Nestorian, Celtic, and others.

Armand Toussaint also played an important role in the creation and development of the Church of the New Covenant founded by his friend Roger Caro. It was indeed Armand Toussaint who ordained Roger Caro Bishop. Later, Roger Caro was to ordain Armand Toussaint, *sub conditione,* a frequent practice in the Gnostic churches.

Armand Toussaint and Martinism

Armand Toussaint was received into Martinism and consecrated Unknown Superior Initiator by his Master Serge Marcotoune of Kiev, Master Hermius, who instructed him to open a Lodge in Belgium. After the death of Serge Marcotoune on January 15, 1971, Armand Toussaint founded the *Ordre Martiniste des Chevaliers du Christ,* a vehicle of both the Russian Martinist lineage and a chivalric lineage. The O.M.C.C. developed little until the 1980s. At that time, Armand Toussaint authorized Triantaphyllos Kotzamanis and Pol Lysis to open lodges with a distinctly Hermetic character, under the name of the Lodges of Green Knights. This current of the O.M.C.C. developed on all continents, and at the beginning of 1994, Armand Toussaint authorized the reorganization of the Lodges of Green Knights under the authority of an International Grand Lodge of the Green Knights, very independent, but remaining in the bosom of the O.M.C.C. Armand Toussaint was also a member of the Order of Knight Masons Elus Coëns of the Universe, but moved away quickly, considering the proposed operations too complex and often ineffective. Although reluctant, he never objected to the relations maintained by the Martinist Lodges of Green Knights with one of the currently operative Elus Coëns orders.

Close to Dr. Lefebure, Armand Toussaint used Phosphenism both on the educational and initiatory levels. Dr. Lefebure had carried out extensive research in cerebral physiology. He demonstrated the deep connection between certain traditional practices and physiological phenomena. Armand Toussaint, who was on the lookout for all scientific innovations, very early on perceived the interest of this work in clarifying traditional practices. Much later, he adopted the same approach with N.L.P., Neuro-Linguistic Programming, before it became of interest to the business community.

Humanism and Ecumenism

Armand Toussaint remained a committed humanist all his life. After the Second World War, he was contacted for the project "Stop War," a spiritual project that attempted, through conferences, international congresses, and publications, to orient national and international policies in a different direction than the one we know. This project received the support of Queen Elizabeth II of England. Not getting any significant results, Armand Toussaint resumed studies of general culture and devoted himself to his spiritual quest. He was also secretary of the World Spiritual Council which worked for an ecumenism without conversion under the presidency of Franz Wittemans, his personal friend. Throughout his life, he showed real tolerance and great wisdom in the face of crises that shake people and societies. He regularly supported projects aimed at creating contacts between the heads of traditional organizations. In a letter dated March 20, 1973, addressed to Roger and Madeleine Caro, he wrote: "My congratulations also on your broad genuine ecumenical sense. Spiritualists of all kinds speak incessantly of brotherhood and of the same one God, without however wanting to meet and dialogue as do all other large established civil or military bodies, despite very different and often even opposing ideologies. We are far from the mark in general." In the last years of his life, no longer able to travel, he approved and followed with interest the ecumenical experience of the Rainbow Symposia and, later, the Group of Thebes.

Armand Toussaint and Astrology

Armand Toussaint was an excellent astrologer. He constructed and interpreted the chart of each postulant for the O.M.C.C., but also, if possible, of each collaborator who was not a member of the Martinist order. His interpretation was always very favorable to the development of the person. He looked for signs of initiatory work and also delivered advice on health, prevention being a constant concern for him. He was also a vegetarian and advised, without imposing it, vegetarianism to the members of the O.M.C.C. and E.R.A.[129] He also used astrology to establish the best conditions for an ordination or an important initiation, as for a delicate alchemical operation.

---

129 *Église Rosicrucienne Apostolique,* the Rosicrucian Apostolic Church.

Armand Toussaint and Alchemy

Armand Toussaint was an operative. He worked in the laboratory. Passionate about Alchemy, his meeting with Roger Caro was decisive for both men and for the organizations they led separately. When Armand Toussaint wrote for the first time to Roger Caro on August 20, 1971, he presented himself in particular as a "student in Alchemy for 25 years, without any real practical realization" and asked to benefit from the teaching of the Elder Brothers of the Rose-Croix. This date therefore saw the birth of a friendship that never faded between the two men, despite time, age, and distance. These were the first steps of Armand Toussaint on the Way of Cinnabar, a path that he explored until the end of his life, to even become one of the best specialists of this path that has a double interest, educational and operative. In particular, he researched all possible medical applications on this path. Close to the East Indian and Chinese paths, he also studied the internal Way of Cinnabar.

In 1992, he authorized the creation of a Martinist Lodge called *Cinabro,* bringing together the Brothers and Sisters of the *Ordre Martiniste des Chevaliers du Christ* who devoted themselves to the study and practice of the Way of Cinnabar. This Lodge is still active.

It does not seem that Armand Toussaint intensively practiced other alchemical ways, despite some contact with Eugene Canseliet as attested by a handwritten letter from Eugene Canseliet addressed to Armand Toussaint dated August 20, 1968.

Armand Toussaint had also received a very precise knowledge of an internal Alchemy of the Body of Glory, based on the Song of Songs, a text he published with a commentary.

Alchemical Synthesis of the Great Work
by Raymond Panaghion

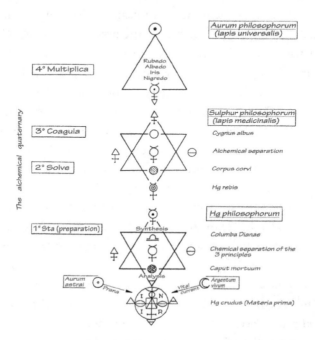

Armand Toussaint and Roger Caro

The meeting of Armand Toussaint with Roger Caro was to be at the origin of the birth of the E.U.N.A., Universal Church of the New Alliance.

When Roger Caro received Armand Toussaint's first letter, he saw it as a sign from Heaven. Indeed, since 1969, the Order of the Elder Brothers of the Rose+Croix no longer had a Grand-Prior General (cf. the letter sent by Roger Caro to Armand Toussaint on September 24, 1971). He therefore offered this post to Armand Toussaint who accepted without hesitation. Roger Caro immediately put him, in accordance with the tradition of the Order, in contact with a Master-guide who assisted him to the Adeptate, which he received in 1972—the Adeptate that made him, in his own right, an Elder Brother of the Rose+Cross. He was later named Honorary Imperator of the F.A.R+C.

Armand Toussaint consecrated Roger Caro Bishop on Saturday, June 10, 1972, in the residence of the Angelots, in Saint-Cyr-sur-Mer, seat of the F.A.R+C. After considering the development of the Rosicrucian Apostolic Church in France and abroad (at that time, the E.R.A. was almost non-existent outside Belgium), Roger Caro proposed to Armand Toussaint to found the Church of the New Covenant in intercommunion with the E.R.A., the first for the alchemists, the second for the Rosicrucians. To found his church, Roger Caro relied on documents from the former Templar Church, canons and rituals, found in the archives of the Order of F.A.R+C. This project was essential for him, and he owed a life of thanks to Armand Toussaint for having allowed him to carry it out (cf. letter of 31 September 1971, sent by Roger Caro to Armand Toussaint and his wife). Later, Roger Caro was to close the Order of F.A.R+C, inviting members to withdraw into the bosom of the Church of the New Covenant.

Armand Toussaint and the East

Armand Toussaint traveled widely. He met several Eastern Masters. He was notably the friend of Swami Sivananda Baraswati. Also a follower of the Soto Zen school, he was in favor of an ecumenism between East and West. He perfected an original technique, known as "panaghion yoga," ranging from the Martinist bases taught by Serge Marcotoune to what he called "fine-tuning," both a technique and a concept that he had received from a lineage of great Indian saints. At the end of his life, he was most curiously referring to the "green and very tangible crystals of the City of Shamballah."

The exceptional man

This brief overview of Armand Toussaint's career in the discreet world of Hermeticism makes it possible to understand the influence of this man with his lively intelligence on many traditional Western currents, and the help he was able provide to numerous seekers, Martinists, Rosicrucians, Freemasons, and Alchemists.

Very rational and pragmatic, having followed the evolution of psychological research up to the end of his days, he was for many the friend, the guide and companion, the Brother, always present in good days as in bad days.

It is therefore to a *Friend of God* that we render a much-deserved homage.

You will find more about Armand Toussaint at this address:

http://incoerismo.files.wordpress.com/2012/01/esprit-des-choses-ns-3.pdf

Appendix 3

Martinism and Modernity[130]

The question of the relationship between Martinism and modernity deserves to be asked regularly. It is a *trompe-l'œil* question and it is precisely the *trompe-l'œil* that makes the question interesting.

But first of all, what Martinism are we talking about?

Let us recall briefly, with Robert Amadou,[131] what the term "Martinism" covers.

It is first the Primitive Cult of the Order of Knight Masons Elus Coëns of the Universe,[132] founded by Martines de Pasqually (1710-1774) of which Louis-Claude de Saint-Martin was the secretary

---

130 Article originally published on the Editions Arqa webzine.

131 See *Martinisme* by Robert Amadou. 2nd revised and expanded edition (Guérigny, Fr: CIREM, 1997).

132 Two books presented and commented on by Robert Amadou are essential to the understanding of the Primitive Cult: *Les leçons de Lyon aux élus coëns. Un cours de martinisme au XVIIIe siècle par Louis-Claude de Saint-Martin, Jean-Jacques Du Roy D'Hauterive, Jean-Baptiste Willermoz* by Robert and Catherine Amadou. First complete edition published from the original manuscripts (Paris: Dervy, 1999); Martines de Pasqually— *Traité sur la réintégration des êtres dans leur première propriété, vertu et puissance spirituelle divine.* First authentic edition based on the manuscript of Louis-Claude de Saint-Martin, established and presented by Robert Amadou (Le Tremblay: Diffusion rosicrucienne, 1995).

and probably the best student.

It is the Theosophy of Louis-Claude de Saint-Martin[133] (1743-1803), at the crossroads of two foundational experiences, the experience of a Réau-Croix who successfully realized all the Coëns operations, and the encounter with the work of Jacob Bœhme of which he became a translator. Recall that Jacob Bœhme, often described as a mystic, was also a high-level operative hermetist. Louis-Claude de Saint-Martin talks to us about Gnosis.

It is the Masonic system of the Rectified Scottish Rite founded by Jean-Baptiste Willermoz (1730-1824) from the Templar Strict Observance,[134] imbued with the doctrine of reintegration of Martines de Pasqually. The Profession and the Grand Profession, the crown of this system, are a synthesis of the doctrine conveyed by the Primitive Cult. The RER is one of the few Masonic systems presenting an overall coherence. It does not suffer, as do a number of Masonic rites, from the circumstantial attachments of this or that grade.

Finally, it is the Martinist Order, and its many emanations, founded in 1887 by Papus (1865-1916). Today, all the Martinist orders constitute a living and influential movement carrying the

---

133 Les Œuvres complètes de Louis-Claude de Saint-Martin are available from Olms. We draw your attention to the introductions of Robert Amadou that enable a better understanding of the thought of the Unknown Philosopher.

134 In 1778, in Lyon, the national convention of the Gauls of the Strict Observance adopted the reform proposed by Willermoz, which makes the Rectified Scottish Rite the heir of the Coën doctrine. The Profession and the Grand Profession, which constitute the secret class of the Rectified Scottish Rite, are responsible for preserving the doctrine of the Primitive Cult. In 1782, at the international convention of the Strict Observance, in Wilhelmsbad, Jean-Baptiste Willermoz and his followers adopted the reform of 1778. The Profession and the Grand Profession officially disappeared. Yet this secret class has continued its work in an occult manner for two centuries.

principles and symbols of Illuminism, principles and symbols that we sought to inscribe a few years ago in a charter: *Charter for XXIst Century Martinist Orders.*

Traditional Martinism, which therefore refers to Louis-Claude de Saint-Martin and Martines de Pasqually, has been expressed in many ways from generation to generation. Today we are experiencing the third wave of the Companions of Hierophany. After the initial companions, Papus and Stanislas de Guaita, the most brilliant of them, came the two Roberts, Robert Ambelain and Robert Amadou, who gave an unprecedented rise to Martinism while deepening its theosophical foundations. With each wave, Martinism continues to expand through its initiatory radiance. It is enriched by new encounters without losing its intrinsic quality, even if we observe here and there some tendencies to scatter or some worldly temptations. Traditional Martinism remains initiatory and is the privileged Illuminist vehicle of the ways of awakening, of realization or (the Martinezist word is essential) of "reintegration."

Every initiatory path leads from dual consciousness to nondual consciousness, from the "person" to the Self, from the "mask" to Christ. With Louis-Claude de Saint-Martin, we will speak of the man (or woman) of the stream, who becomes a man of desire, to engender the new man and, finally, by a redeification, to manifest his original and ultimate nature as the man of spirit and assume the ultimate ministry. We rediscover the quadrant of the ways of awakening as we have established on multiple occasions.

The ways of awakening, all traditions combined, can be broken down into four modalities that determine four relations with the Real.

If the quester immediately grasps that he is the Absolute (the Absolute simultaneously grasping him), the quest is over, here and now, forever. It hasn't started at all—everything is accomplished. The word "Absolute" can be replaced by the word "God," the ultimate personal pronoun. The Absolute is also the All, the One, the Great Real, it does not matter what word is used, provided that we understand it as the Self.

The Absolute is first of all Absolute Freedom. The manifestation of this Freedom leads the Absolute to forget itself in the multiplicity of forms that it creates, to lose itself the better to find itself, to recognize itself, to deny its own nature in the Great Game, the game of Consciousness and Energy.

If he does not grasp the Absolute, but perceives the Game of Consciousness and Energy, Christ/Shekinah, Absolute/Existence, the quester is the player himself, the one who is played within duality without ever, in the background, leaving joy, the bliss of nondual consciousness. He is simultaneously all the pairs of opposites without ever identifying with one of the two terms of the opposition.

If the Game of Consciousness and Energy remains foreign to the quester, then he respects the rites and the rules (the absolute Rule being the absence of rule and the infinite Freedom). He studies their myths, symbols, and arcana until behind the traditional forms he distinguishes what will appear to him as an absolute structure, an archetype of traditional forms, an energetic vessel navigating the ocean of Consciousness. This absolute structure then reveals itself as the memory trace of the Game of Energy and Consciousness, a trace left "hollow" in Silence, which can be considered, metaphorically, as a virgin substance.

The crossing of dual forms and, among them, traditional forms leads to the Land of Silence, of non-representation, to the "Central Earth," to the "High Country of the Friends of God."

If the quester does not understand the rites, if the rites do not make sense to him, then he devotes himself to Beneficence, which Robert Amadou said is the equivalent of theurgy. He puts himself at the service of otherness. He serves his neighbor whom he believes to be other, while the true "neighbor," the one who approaches, is the one who springs forth, free from all hindrance, in himself, the Self.

This said, we can question modernity. Should we not talk about actuality, the actuality of appearance, of what presents itself, of the situation? Indeed, in the speech of the specialist who specializes in speech, we no longer know whether we are confronted with modernity, post-modernity, post-post-modernity, or any other concept. But what strikes the observer of the world of initiation is that many women and men of desire suffer from the apparent inadequacy, the impossible compromise, between the spirit of tradition and the environment, cultural and intellectual, in which we evolve. The issues between tradition and modernity, between initiation and education, are not specific to our time, but seem to crystallize today in an acute crisis, which is no longer thought, which is unthinkable, but a perverse unthinkable. While in the past, the issue of tradition and modernity had evolved into a fruitful dialectic, authorized by the ritual separation between the sacred and the profane, today thought freezes in a heavy and sterile face-off. But, on closer inspection, the human being on the quest does not suffer more from modernity than does the layman. Both feel dislocated, dislodged, out of line, thrown back into the peripheries of a game they do not want to join, caught in a speeding accident. Let us note that we are indeed inscribed in the game of the dual consciousness that separates, opposes, divides, and is lost in the jubilation of acceleration.

Another relationship can be established with modernity: an initiatory relationship. There are no initiatory objects versus non-initiatory objects. For a long time philosophy considered that certain objects were not philosophical. Fortunately, those times are over. Similarly, it is effective to consider that it is not the object that is initiatory, but the relationship maintained with the object. We can establish an initiatory relationship with any object that presents itself in consciousness. Modernity, and its procession of experiences that tend to distance us from ourselves, is only one object, one element of the situation among others. Modernity is just another name given to what is woven in the opacity of consciousness by the superimpositions of the ego.

The question of tradition and modernity then appears as a *trompe-l'œil.* It hides the real question of our inability to be silent, to be nothing, to extricate ourselves from the conditioning and artifices of the person for whom so-called modernity is just another avatar.

From a nondual point of view, what matters lies in our power of verticality, our ability to inscribe everything that presents itself, tradition along with modernity, all the antinomies that constitute the markers of dual precedence, in the nondual silence of Being. To leave the stream of a consciousness identified with forms to allow the Spirit to live in oneself, to let Gnosis (Knowledge in oneself, by oneself) flow without grasping anything, without holding anything back. It is an art that requires skill and the intuition of ones own intrinsic freedom. It is an art that unfolds in what Henri Corbin calls the imaginal. What happens, what presents itself, symbolizes what is really played out in consciousness. Everything becomes material for the work of reintegration. Let us establish in this imaginal the mysterious scenario, both traditional and strangely modern, of *Le Crocodile ou la guerre du bien contre le mal,* a key text established by Louis-Claude de Saint-Martin.

Louis-Claude de Saint-Martin was embedded in his time, which does not detract from his lucidity. An aristocrat, he became fascinated by the ideas and principles of the French Revolution before regretting their excesses.

Robert Amadou, our elder Brother, demonstrated, in a way that could sometimes make certain narrow egos smile, how, on a daily basis, a Martinist, a Gnostic (consider the two words as synonyms), who practices the imitation of Saint-Martin, this other Christ, at the same time allies himself with modernity and frees himself from it as soon as he lives and realizes himself as a new man and manifests the ministry of the man of spirit, the man free of all limitation. Let us remember his silhouette in a cassock at his beloved Sorbonne. If there was uneasiness, it was in those who were locked in a straitjacket of prejudices, not in the free conscience of those who live here and now in the place of the Heart. Robert Amadou was a man of tradition within modernity itself, never against modernity. The Martinist is a monk in the world, not a monk despite the world or against the world. He belongs to the invisible Gnostic Monastery,[135] at the assembly of itinerant initiates who make themselves invisible and impersonal in the world through the operative practice of the mask and the cloak, leaving visible only their works, large or modest. The nondual relationship maintained by the monk (the one who is alone because he is one) with every object that presents itself in the consciousness, thing, feeling, emotion, or concept... frees him from all form, empties the dualistic principle of separation symbolized by Satan of all vitality, and establishes Christ in Glory, the absolute and free nondual consciousness.

If behind the question of the relationship between Martinism and modernity, we want to pose the question of the future of

---

135   The invisible Gnostic Monastery is not merely a concept, however attractive, but a rigorous practice. Today it is implemented, nonexclusively, within the framework of the Rosicrucian Apostolic and Gnostic Church founded by Armand Toussaint in his time.

Martinism,[136] we will then agree to say that this does not depend on the times in which it is embedded, but on the relationship maintained with the times. It is therefore just as likely that the times to come will be favorable or hostile to tradition. The Spirit remains.

It is enough for the Martinist to lose the Holy Spirit to find it.

---

136 In a recent conference, some speakers asked the question of the future of Martinism. Some saw it as very Masonic. It would then have been necessary to ask what is the future of Freemasonry, in the sense of its initiatory future, because no one can doubt the worldly future of the Masonic institution. Freemasonry, as respectable as it is, is not an initiatory organization. Its original project is spiritual, political, and societal, not initiatory. This is why the multiple initiatory grafts are invariably rejected. They leave traces, however, and those remain as useful indications. If Papus thought of Martinism as a means of perfecting Freemasonry, we can now doubt this possibility, as Freemasonry is stuck, cannibalized by secular worldliness. Martinism will always benefit, institutionally, by standing at a respectful distance from its somewhat bulimic cousin.

Appendix 4

Hymn to the Unknown Saints

All you, saints of oblivion
Anonymous by erasure
Or adepts of the shadow
Who preferred the hidden to the light
In order to accomplish the work without noise
Unknown saints
Unknown silents
Unknown superiors
Who preferred blame
To the recognition of men
You nameless
Who watch over the masterless
The casteless and other untouchables
You who solicit neither gilding nor powers
Neither prayers nor sacrifices
To guard the Holy City
To introduce the pilgrims
Without discrimination
Beneficent knights
Who renounced the sword
Armor and shield

But not the psychopomp horse
In order to connect the black earth
To the red sun
And take root in Heaven
All you, without churches
Who have the world as a temple
Saints of the simple and the banal
Prophets of unknown peoples
To the human senses
I salute you
I ask nothing of you
I know that where I am, you are
That where you are, I am
That we are, together
The ones we dream of
To better *Remember* us.

Saint-Martinian Bibliography

Louis-Claude de Saint-Martin

Œuvres majeures Collection by Georg Olms, facsimiles of the original editions with introduction and notes by Robert Amadou:

- I—*Des erreurs et de la vérité* (facsimile ed., 1775). [Published in English as *Of Errors and Truth*. Bayonne, NJ: Rose Circle, 2017.]
  + *Ode sur l'origine et la destination de l'homme* (1781)
- II—*Le Tableau naturel des rapports qui existent entre Dieu, l'homme et l'univers* (facsimile of 1782). [Published in English as *Natural Table*. Bayonne, NJ: Rose Circle, 2018.]
  + *Discours sur la meilleure manière de rappeler à la raison les nations livrées aux erreurs et aux superstitions* (1783)
- III—*L'Homme de désir* (facsimile ed., 1802). [To be published in English as *Man of Desire*. Bayonne, NJ: Rose Circle, forthcoming.]
- IV—*Ecce homo* (facsimile edition of 1792).
  + *Le Nouvel Homme* (facsimile ed. An IV, 1792). [To be published in English as *The New Man*. Bayonne, NJ: Rose Circle, forthcoming.]
- V—vol. 1—*De l'esprit des choses*, t. 1 (facsimile ed. An VIII, 1800)
- V—vol. 2—*De l'esprit des choses*, t. 2 (facsimile ed. An VIII, 1800)
  + *Controverse avec Garat* (facsimile of 1801)

- VI—*Le Ministère de l'homme-esprit* (facsimile of 1802). [Published in English as *Man, His True Nature and Ministry*. London: W.H. Allen, 1864.]
- VII—*Poésies, Écrits politiques*, Paris 1795-1797.

Uncollected:

- *Controverse avec Garat, précédée d'autres écrits philosophiques*, Corpus des œuvres de philosophie en langue française. Paris: Fayard, 1990.
- *Mon livre vert*, text prepared and published in full for the first time by Robert Amadou. Paris: Cariscript, 1991.
- *Le Crocodile ou la guerre du bien et du mal*. Paris: Triades, 1962.
- *Mon portrait historique et philosophique (1789-1803)*, published by Robert Amadou. Paris: Julliard, 1961.
- *Les nombres*. Nice: Bélisane, 1983.

Martinism

- *Les hommes de désir: Entretiens sur le martinisme* by Serge Caillet and Xavier Cuvelier-Roy. Grenoble: Le Mercure Dauphinois, 2012.
- *Martinisme* by Robert Amadou. 2nd augmented edition. Guérigny: CIREM, 1997.
- *Le martinisme* by Robert Ambelain. Paris: Niclaus, 1946.
- *Illuminisme et contre-illuminisme* by Robert Amadou. Paris: Cariscript, 1989.
- *L'occultisme, esquisse d'un monde vivant* by Robert Amadou. Saint-Jean-de-la-Ruelle: Chanteloup, 1987.
- *Le Martinisme. L'enseignement secret des Maîtres* by Jean-Marc Vivenza. Grenoble: Le Mercure Dauphinois, 2006.
- *La Prière du Cœur selon Louis-Claude de Saint-Martin, dit le Philosophe Inconnu* by Jean-Marc Vivenza. La Bégude de Mazenc: Arma Artis, 2007.
- *L'Église et le sacerdoce selon Louis-Claude de Saint-Martin* by

Jean-Marc Vivenza. Hyères: La Pierre Philosophale, 2013.

- *Le culte « en esprit » de l'Église intérieure* by Jean-Marc Vivenza. Hyères: La Pierre Philosophale, 2014.
- *Le mystère de l'Église intérieure ou la « naissance » de Dieu dans l'âme* by Jean-Marc Vivenza. Hyères: La Pierre Philosophale, 2016.
- *Régénération et création littéraire chez Louis-Claude de Saint-Martin* by Jean-Louis Ricard. Guérigny: CIREM, 1996.
- *Étude sur Le Crocodile ou la guerre du bien et du mal de Louis-Claude de Saint-Martin* by Jean-Louis Ricard. Guérigny: CIREM, 2002.
- *Maximes et pensées* by Louis-Claude de Saint-Martin. Paris: André Silvaire, 1963.
- *Cours de martinisme* by Serge Caillet. Les Auberts: Institute Eléazar. 1990-2008.
- *Belle Rose* by Renée de Brimont. Contributions by Serge Caillet, Michelle Nahon & Maurice Friot, Francis Laget. Aubagne: Éditions de la Tarente, 2016.
- *Les Cahiers de la Tour Saint Jacques*, special issue dedicated to Louis-Claude de Saint-Martin. Paris: 3rd quarter 1961.
- *Les Cahiers de la Tour Saint Jacques*, dedicated to Illuminism in the 18th century. Paris: 2nd, 3rd and 4th quarters 1960.
- *L'Esprit des Choses,* First series nos. 1 to 33. Guérigny: CIREM, 1992-2002.
- *Le martinisme contemporain et ses véritables origines* by Robert Ambelain, article published in *Les Cahiers Destin.* Paris: 1948.
- *Martinisme et Martinézisme. Doctrine Générale* by Robert Ambelain, article published in *L'Initiation.* Paris: January-February, 1953.
- *Une Initiation martiniste sous l'occupation* by Robert Ambelain, article published in *L'Initiation.* Paris: March-April 1953.
- *Technique de la voie cardiaque* by Robert Ambelain, article published in *L'Initiation.* Paris: July-September, 1962.

Order of Knight Masons Elus Coëns of the Universe

- *Les leçons de Lyon aux élus coëns. Un cours de martinisme au XVIIIe siècle par Louis-Claude de Saint-Martin, Jean-Jacques Du Roy D'Hauterive, Jean-Baptiste Willermoz.* Robert and Catherine Amadou. First complete edition published from the original manuscripts. Paris: Dervy, 1999.
- *Traite sur la réintégration des êtres dans leur première propriété, vertu et puissance spirituelle divine* by Martines de Pasqually. First authentic edition based on the manuscript of Louis-Claude de Saint-Martin, prepared and presented by Robert Amadou. Le Tremblay: Diffusion rosicrucienne 1995. [Abridged editions published in English as *Treatise Concerning the Reintegration of Beings* (Toronto: Johannine Press, 2001), and as *Treatise on the Reintegration of Beings* (Sunderland, UK: Septentrione, 2007).]
- *Angéliques,* Volume 1 and 2, by Catherine and Robert Amadou. First complete edition from the manuscripts of Louis-Claude de Saint-Martin. Guérigny: CIREM, 2001.
- *La magie des Élus Coëns. Théurgie. Instruction secrète. Fonds Z. Les manuscrits réservés du Philosophe inconnu.* Published by Robert Amadou. Paris: Cariscript, 1988.
- *Le Temple Cohen de Toulouse (1760-1792): Michel Taillefer, Les disciples toulousains de Martines de Pasqually et de Saint-Martin suivi de Fragments extraits de diverses lettres ayant en vue les vraies connaissances (1776-1780) colligés par Joseph Du Bourg,* published by Robert Amadou. Paris: Cariscript, 1986.
- *Les sept sceaux des élus coëns* by Serge Caillet. Grenoble: Le Mercure Dauphinois, 2011.
- *Judéo-christianisme, théurgie et franc-maçonnerie au XVIIIe siècle: l'Ordre des chevaliers maçons élus coëns de l'univers* by Serge Caillet. Paris: SFERE, 2014.
- *Le Manuscrit d'Alger,* the first complete serial edition of the fac-

simile, with partial transcription, of the original from the Bibliothèque nationale de France, *L'Esprit des Choses*. First series nos. 13-14 to 29-30. Guérigny: CIREM, 1996-2001. [Published in English in two volumes as *The Green Book of the Élus Coëns*. London: Hell Fire Club, 2020.]

* *Le Grand Manuscrit d'Alger*, volumes I to III, edited by Georges Courts. Marseille: Arqa, 2009-2017.

Rectified Scottish Rite

* *L'Homme-Dieu. Traité des deux natures* by Jean-Baptiste Willermoz followed by *Le mystère de la Trinité* according to Louis-Claude de Saint-Martin. La Tremblay: Diffusion rosicrucienne, 1999.

* *Archives secrètes de la Franc-maçonnerie* by Steel-Maret, Geneva: Slatkine, 2012.

* *Structure des rituels maçonniques des trois premiers grades du Rite Écossais Rectifié* (4 volumes) by Raymond E. F. Guillaume. Toulouse: University of Toulouse—Le Mirail, Department of Modern History, October 1993.

* *Temple et contemplation* by Henry Corbin, preface by Gilbert Durand. Paris: Entre Lacs, 2006. [Published in English as *Temple and Contemplation*. London: KPI, 1986.]

* *Les élus coëns et le Régime Écossais Rectifié* by Jean-Marc Vivenza. Grenoble: Le Mercure Dauphinois, 2010.

* *René Guénon et le Rite Écossais Rectifié* by Jean-Marc Vivenza. Paris: Simorgh, 2007.

* *La Franc-maçonnerie à la lumière du Verbe. Le Régime Écossais Rectifié* by Jean-François Var. Paris: Dervy, 2013.

* *Présence du Rite Écossais Rectifié* by Yves Saez. Paris: Dervy, 2010.

* *Principes et problèmes spirituels du Rite Écossais Rectifié* by Jean Tourniac. Paris: Dervy, 1969.

- *L'aventure du Rite Écossais Rectifié* by Jean-Claude Sitbon. Volume I: *Approche historique.* Volume II: *De Tubalcaïn à Phaleg.* Aubagne: Éditions de la Tarente, 2015.
- *La Doctrine de la Réintégration des êtres* by Jean-Marc Vivenza. Hyères: La Pierre Philosophale, 2012.
- *Regards sur les Temples de la Franc-maçonnerie* by Camille Savoire, text edited by Jean-Marc Vivenza. Archives and Masonic Documents collection. Hyères: La Pierre Philosophale, 2015.
- *Chevalerie, Franc-Maçonnerie et Spiritualité—Exercices Spirituels pour les Ours et les Chevaliers* by Michel Bédaton and Rémi Boyer, bilingual Franco-Portuguese edition. Illustrations by Jean-Michel Nicollet. Guérigny, France: CIREM; Sintra, Portugal: Zefiro and Arcane Zero, 2015.
- *Le Régime Écossais Rectifié, de la Doctrine de la Réintégration à l'Imago Templi* by Rémi Boyer. Prefaces by Serge Caillet and José Anes. Aubagne: Éditions de la Tarente, 2015. [To be published in English as *The Rectified Scottish Rite: From the Doctrine of Reintegration to the* Imago Templi. Bayonne, NJ: Rose Circle, forthcoming 2022.]
- *La Grande Profession: documents et découvertes, le fonds Turckheim,* Renaissance Traditionnelle, nos. 181-182. Clichy: January-April 2016.
- *La naissance de la Province d'Auvergne du Régime Rectifié d'après la correspondance de Jean-Baptiste Willermoz (1772-1775)* by Loïc Montanella. Aubagne: Éditions de la Tarente, 2016.

Jacob Bœhme

- *Les trois Principes de l'Essence Divine.* La Bégude de Mazenc: Arma Artis, 2007. [Published in English as *The Three Principles of the Divine Essence.* Chicago: Yogi Publication Society, 1909.]
- *Le chemin pour aller au Christ.* Milan: Archè, 2004. [Published in English as *The Way to Christ.* New York: Paulist Press, 1978.]

- *Le Livre des Sacrements.* Milan: Archè, 1990. [Published in English as *Of Christ's Testaments.* London: H. Blunden, 1652.]
- *Clef ou explication des divers points et termes principaux de la vie et de la mort.* Milan: Archè, 1977. [Published in English as *The Clavis or Key.* London: H. Blunden, 1647.]
- *De l'Election, de la Grâce ou de la Volonté de Dieu envers les Hommes.* Paris: L'Age d'Homme, 1976. [Published in English as *Concerning the Election of Grace.* London: H. Blunden, 1655.]
- *De la signature des choses.* Milan: Archè, 1975. [Published in English as *Signatura Rerum.* London: H. Blunden, 1651.]
- *Mysterium Magnum.* Paris: Aubier, 1945. [Published in English as *Mysterium Magnum.* London: H. Blunden, 1654.]

Emmanuel Swedenborg

- *Arcanes célestes* by Emmanuel Swedenborg. Printed by Mme Ve Dondey-Dupre. Paris: Librairie de la Nouvelle Jérusalem, 1841-1885. [Published in English as *Arcana Cœlestia,* Redesigned Standard Edition. West Chester, PA: Swedenborg Foundation, 1998.]
- *Les délices de la Sagesse sur l'Amour conjugal* by Emmanuel Swedenborg. Paris: Librairie de la Nouvelle Jérusalem, 1887. [Published in English as *Love in Marriage: The Sensible Joy in Married Love and the Foolish Pleasures of Illicit Love.* West Chester, PA: Swedenborg Foundation, 1992.]
- *Du Ciel et de l'Enfer* by Emmanuel Swedenborg. Paris: Librairie Fischbacher, 1899. [Published in English as *Heaven and Hell,* New Century Edition. West Chester, PA: Swedenborg Foundation, 2000.]
- *Les quatre doctrines principales de la Nouvelle Jérusalem* by Emmanuel Swedenborg. Paris: Librairie Fischbacher, 1904. [Published in English as *The Shorter Works of 1763,* New Century Edition. West Chester, PA: Swedenborg Foundation, 2020.]

- *La Franc-maçonnerie swedenborgienne* by Serge Caillet. Aubagne: Éditions de la Tarente, 2015.

Theurgy

- *L'Anacrise pour avoir la communication avec son bon ange gardien* by Robert Amadou. Paris: Cariscript, 1988.

Gnosis

- *Écrits gnostiques* under the direction of Jean-Pierre Mahé and Paul-Hubert Poirier. Paris: Bibliothéque de la Pléiade, 2007.
- *Introduction à la littérature gnostique I, collections retrouvées avant 1945* by Michel Tardieu and Jean-Daniel Dubois. Paris: Cerf and CNRS, 1986.
- *Les enseignements secrets de la Gnose* by T. Simon (Albert de Pouvourville) and T. Théophane (Léon Champrenaud). Milan: Archè, 1999.
- *De la Chevalerie au secret du Temple* by Jean Tourniac. Paris: Dervy, 2008.
- *Le Grand Œuvre comme fondement d'une spiritualité laïque. Le chemin vers l'Individuation* by Claude Bruley. Cordes sur Ciel: Rafael de Surtis, 2008.

Master Philippe of Lyon

- *Monsieur Philippe « l'Ami de Dieu »* by Serge Caillet, second edition. Paris: Dervy, 2013.
- *Vie et paroles du Maître Philippe,* testimony of Alfred Haehl. Paris: Dervy, 1990.
- *Le Maître Philippe de Lyon,* commented by Sri Sevananda. Paris: Cariscript, 1984.
- *Philippe de Lyon, médecin, thaumaturge et conseiller du tsar* by Renée-Paule Guillot. Paris: Les Deux Océans, 1994.

Autour du Maître Philippe Collection from Mercure Dauphinois

- *Mes Souvenirs* by Claude Laurent. Grenoble: 2003.
- *La Vie Inconnue de Jésus-Christ* by Sedir. Grenoble: 2003.
- *Les Réponses de Maître Philippe* by Auguste Jacquot and Auguste Philippe. Grenoble: 2004.
- *L'Esprit qui peut tout* by G. Phaneg. Grenoble: 2004.
- *Confirmation de l'Évangile* by Jean-Baptiste Ravier. Grenoble: 2005.
- *Monsieur Philippe de Lyon* by Philippe Collin. Grenoble: 2005.
- *Vie et Enseignement de Jean Chapas* by Philippe Collin. Grenoble: 2005.
- *Les carnets de Victoire Philippe* by Victoire Philippe. Grenoble: 2007.
- *Le chien du Berger,* a film by Bernard Bonnamour. Grenoble: 2007.

CPSIA information can be obtained
at www.ICGtesting.com
Printed in the USA
LVHW050736260321
682548LV00022B/644